SALADE

PASCALE BEALE

SALADE

Recipes from the Market Table

Foreword by

TRACEY RYDER

Published by

M27 Editions LLC
3030 State Street
Santa Barbara, California 93105
PHONE (805) 563-0099
FAX (805) 563-2070
EMAIL publish@m27editions.com
WEB www.m27editions.com

For cooking classes and merchandise:
WEB www.pascaleskitchen.com
EMAIL info@pascaleskitchen.com

SALADE: Recipes from the Market Table
by Pascale Beale

Second Edition

ISBN: 9780965922777
Library of Congress Catalog Number: 2013955929

Design and Production by Media 27, Inc., Santa Barbara, California

WWW.MEDIA27.COM

Printed and Bound in China

For Harriet and Nancy

Merci mes amies

Contents

Foreword

AS SOMEONE WHO IS A PASSIONATE cook and cookbook collector, I have great respect and admiration for the journey an author takes on their way to creating an extraordinary cookbook. And when that cookbook captures a single subject in its entirety, the end result is something akin to a memorable song, complete with lyrics, melody and chorus, all perfectly gathered together into a pleasing whole. In *Salade: Recipes from the Market Table*, by Pascale Beale, that pleasing whole is made up of deliciously lovely studies on the salad in its countless forms.

Single-subject cookbooks are an important part of our culinary canon because they allow for deeper exploration into a topic from every possible angle — *Salade* is no exception. Throughout the beautifully photographed pages, Pascale inspires us to think about salads in many ways: as daily rituals, healthy side dishes, or as hearty meals that can feed a crowd.

Divided into chapters that are nicely organized by ingredient, such as Green Salads; Apples and Pears; Endive & Fennel; Grains and Rice; Nectarines, Peaches and Plums; and Lentils, Potatoes and Roasted Vegetables, I found myself turning pages quickly, excitedly anticipating the next recipe — each one a creative example of just how versatile salads can be. And no one can dispute the extra benefit of salads as relatively low-calorie, vegetable-packed deliciousness, especially when filled with seasonal ingredients picked at the peak of ripeness.

There are shining stars you will turn to seasonally, such as the Heirloom Tomato Salad in summer (who could resist?), but the Green Tomato and Grilled Zucchini Salad is not to be missed either. The same goes for Pascale's Birthday Beet Salad, the Fingerling Potato and Bacon Salad and the Smoked Salmon Salad. But the salad that struck me most, partly for its utter freshness and simplicity but also because of the very personal and endearing head note that leads it off, is Petite Salade Verte:

Tracey Ryder is cofounder of Edible Communities — a network of nearly 80 regional food magazines — and winner of the James Beard Publication of the Year Award.

"It all began with this salad. This is the salad my grandmother made every day. It's the salad we ate at home, and it's the first salad I learnt how to make. She would painstakingly rinse the greens, dry the leaves delicately in a tea towel and assemble it just a couple of minutes before dinner. Sometimes she'd add chives, which she would cut with scissors hanging from a hook underneath her kitchen cabinets, kept specifically for that purpose. It was so simple and refreshing..."

I plan to make this salad a daily ritual at my own family's table from now on. Perhaps if I am able to prepare it just right, we will be lucky enough to be transported to Pascale's grandmother's kitchen every now and then. After all, what better thing to incorporate into our busy lives than something so simple and refreshing, and that also creates lasting memories?

Cheers and good eating,
Tracey Ryder

Introduction

I THINK I FIRST BECAME aware of salads — beyond the classic green salad with a mustard vinaigrette we ate almost daily — when I tasted a fabulous, garlicky Caesar salad in a London restaurant decades ago. The restaurant was a very hip, American-style place, complete with bare brick interior, polished wooden floors, black and white photos on the walls and located in a basement. It was cool. I liked to think I was too, sitting at the white paper-covered tables ordering "modern" food. It was there that I first discovered the classics such as Waldorf salad and chopped salad and an exotic sounding vinaigrette called "green goddess." Of course some of those salads were created a century prior, but I didn't know that then. Over the last thirty-plus years, I have explored different types of salads, their origins and history, and I realized that what we think of as new has actually been around for a very long time.

In 1799, John Evelyn published the first English-language cookbook dedicated solely

to salads, *Acetaria: A Discourse on Sallets*. He championed eating greens of all sorts, despite the eighteenth-century English preference for grains and odiferous meats. He directed his readers to "dress their salads with oil of a pallid olive ... such as [from] native Lucca olives," encouraged the use of the best vinegar available, suggested adding fine crystals of salt and recommended mixing common lettuces with mache, spinach, arugula, endive, fennel, radish and nasturtiums. This could have been written today.

I grew up with the classic salad my French grandparents preferred: simple mixed greens with a few herbs, lightly dressed and always served after the main course and before the cheese platter. The only salad they would eat as a first course — or on rare occasions as a main course — was a *Salade Niçoise*. They regarded the modern trend for *salade composé* or salads filled with unusual ingredients (fruit and nuts for example) as some bizarre newfangled fad. Yet these types of salads have their roots in ancient Rome. In Columella's epic work, *De Re Rustica*, he describes a salad of fresh mint, cilantro, leeks, parsley, thyme and fresh cheese, dressed with olive oil, vinegar, salt and pepper. What could be more modern?

Despite a few odd passages in the history of salads — the horrors of molded Jell-O salads (a wiggling form of lime green, filled with suspended olives and tomatoes and decorated with mayonnaise comes to mind) foisted upon the masses in the 1950s — salads have thankfully emerged into creative and delicious amalgams reflective of the twenty-first century. Now a new blend of cultures from around the world inspires more global menus and influences our everyday cooking and eating.

Tabouleh, the Middle Eastern herb and bulgur salad, is now ubiquitous, as is Salade Niçoise, the tuna, green bean, tomato and egg speciality from Nice. Asian and African spices such as chermoula, za'atar, ras al hanout, curry leaves, kokum, Sichuan pepper, wasabi and tamarind have become more readily available. Our local farmers' markets are now filled with daikon, mung beans, bok choy, Chinese cabbage and more. Farmers who immigrated from Laos, Vietnam and Cambodia, as well as those from South Asia, Central and South America and other parts of the world, brought with them a tradition of growing vegetables native to their own cultures. In turn, these ingredients have become part of our own new culinary heritage — a trend that will continue to grow as the migration of people around the world proliferates.

The farmers' markets, full of so many diverse foods, are truly the source of inspiration for my salads. I might spy a new crop of Fuyu persimmons in October, which will entice me to make mache salad with these delicious fruits; or the beautifully colored heirloom tomatoes of August and September, which need nothing more than fruity olive oil, a pinch of salt and some fresh basil leaves to make a salad that mimics a summer sunset; or a new crop of asparagus, fava beans and peas in the spring to send me rushing home for a salad bowl to pop them all into.

The fundamentals of salad making depend on two simple things: excellent, fresh ingredients (preferably local), and, as Oscar Wilde once said, "To make a good salad is to be a brilliant diplomat — the problem is entirely the same in both cases. To know exactly how much oil one must put with one's vinegar." To that end, I have put together some simple vinaigrettes

that will dress your salads brilliantly. Try to find good, fruity, first cold-pressed olive oil to make your vinaigrettes, along with some coarse sea salt and spicy black pepper, such as Tellicherry peppercorns. You will taste the difference.

There are few foods that I would happily eat every day of the year. Salad is one of them. I enjoy the ease with which they can be put together, the endless variations — from light mixed greens to more substantial salad-as-a-meal types, and the fact that I always feel so good when I eat them. I hope when you make any of my *salades* that you will enjoy them too.

Salad Basics

This is the method I use for making almost all of the salads in this book. It is quick and simple, and you only need one bowl. This basic recipe will make enough vinaigrette for a salad for 6-8 people.

Ingredients

3 tablespoons extra virgin olive oil (use first cold pressed if possible)

1 tablespoon vinegar

Pinch of sea salt

Freshly ground black pepper

1

Pour the olive oil and vinegar into a large salad bowl. Add the salt and 2–3 grinds of black pepper into the bowl. Whisk together to form an emulsion.

2

Place salad utensils over the vinaigrette.

3

Place the salad greens on top of the utensils, ensuring that they do not fall into the vinaigrette. They will wilt if left in the vinaigrette for too long. Leave the salad in the bowl, without tossing it, until you are ready to serve.

4

When ready to serve the salad, use the utensils and toss the greens well.

Vinaigrettes

Simple Vinaigrette

3 tablespoons olive oil

1 tablespoon red wine vinegar

Pinch of sea salt

4–5 grinds of black pepper

Combine all the ingredients in a small bowl and whisk together vigorously to form an emulsion.

Refrigerated, this vinaigrette will keep for 2 weeks. If it separates, re-whisk it to recreate the emulsion. This vinaigrette can be used on all green salads. Use a lighter vinegar (white wine or perhaps an apple cider) when serving with delicate greens, such as mache (lamb's lettuce) or butter lettuce. Use a more robust vinegar, such as Jerez or balsamic when serving heartier greens, such as mesclun, dandelion, arugula or spinach.

Lemon Vinaigrette

3 tablespoons olive oil

Zest and juice of 1 lemon

1 teaspoon white wine vinegar

Pinch of sea salt

2–3 grinds of white pepper

Whisk all of the ingredients together to create a smooth emulsion.

Refrigerated, this vinaigrette will keep for 3–4 days. Shake well before using. This vinaigrette is delicious served with chicken salads, and salads with fennel, apples, celery and endives.

Mustard Vinaigrette

1 tablespoon Dijon mustard

1/4 cup olive oil

1 tablespoon red wine vinegar or fig balsamic vinegar

Pinch of sea salt and black pepper

Combine the mustard, olive oil and vinegar in the bottom of a large salad bowl and whisk together to form a thick emulsion. Add a little salt and pepper, and whisk again.

This vinaigrette has the consistency of a light mayonnaise. It is excellent with potato or egg salads, tuna salads or mixed green salads.

Tomato Vinaigrette

¼ cup olive oil

Zest and juice of 1 lemon

1 large red tomato or 6-7 cherry tomatoes — chopped

Pinch of sea salt

Black pepper

Purée all the ingredients in a food processor or blend using an immersion blender in a tall cylinder until you have a smooth vinaigrette. It will have the consistency of a light mayonnaise.

This vinaigrette is fresh and fruity. It is delicious with most green salads and salads that have feta or goat cheese in them. Refrigerated, it will keep for 2-3 days.

Pesto Vinaigrette

¼ cup olive oil

½ bunch cilantro — chopped

½ bunch basil — chopped

1 tablespoon chives — chopped

Juice and zest of 1 lemon

Juice and zest of 1 lime

Pinch of sea salt

Black pepper

Place all of the ingredients in a blender or food processor. Purée until you have a smooth pesto.

This is a zesty vinaigrette that works well with potatoes, pasta, over asparagus and with roasted vegetables. You can store this in the fridge for 3-4 days.

Juice Vinaigrette

⅓ cup carrot juice

⅓ cup orange juice

⅓ cup golden beet juice

⅓ cup olive oil

1 tablespoon white wine vinegar

Pinch of sea salt

Black pepper

Combine all the ingredients in a bowl and whisk together well. This is a fairly thin vinaigrette so a little goes a long way.

If you don't use it immediately, you might have to whisk it again as it may separate a little. Refrigerated, this will keep for 2-3 days. It's wonderful with carrot salads, vegetable salads and with kale and spinach salads.

These vinaigrettes are used throughout the book with slight variations depending on the salad. There are others (avocado, blue cheese and yogurt, for example) that I use for specific salads. These are listed in the index under vinaigrettes.

GREEN SALADS

Petite Salade Verte

—

Salade Verte aux Herbes

—

Salade Mesclun

—

Winter Greens Salad
with Goat Cheese
and Herbs

—

Mache Salad with a
Pomegranate Vinaigrette

—

Mache Salad with
Bresaola and Goat Cheese

—

Wilted Spinach Salad
with Preserved Lemons

—

Arugula Salad with
Shaved Pecorino and
Caramelized Onions

—

Fairview Gardens
Arugula, Spinach and
Dandelion Salad

—

Spring Salad with
Goat Cheese Crostini

—

Mustard Greens,
Mint, Date and
Manchego Salad

—

Kale and Spinach Salad
with Honeyed Shallots
and Plums

Petite Salade Verte

It all began with this salad. This is the salad my grandmother made every day. It's the salad we ate at home, and it's the first salad I learnt how to make. She would painstakingly rinse the greens, dry the leaves delicately in a tea towel and assemble it just a couple of minutes before dinner. Sometimes she'd add chives, which she would cut with scissors hanging from a hook underneath her kitchen cabinets, kept specifically for that purpose. It was so simple and refreshing.

The key is getting absolutely fresh salad greens. Mix your greens or use only one type — it all works. I like adding butter lettuce to this simple salad. The leaves are crisp yet soft, their texture a nice counterpoint to other greens.

Serves 8 people

1 shallot — peeled and very finely diced

2 teaspoons Dijon mustard

3 tablespoons olive oil

1 tablespoon cider vinegar or other light vinegar of your choice

Sea salt and black pepper to taste

12 oz mixed salad greens

1 Place the diced shallot with a pinch of salt in a small bowl and stir to combine. Set aside for 5 minutes.

2 Place the mustard in a large salad bowl. Slowly drizzle in the olive oil and vinegar, and whisk until the vinaigrette resembles the consistency of a light mayonnaise. Add salt and pepper to taste. Toss in the diced shallot and stir to combine. Place salad servers over the vinaigrette.

3 Add the mixed greens to the salad bowl, on top of the servers. When you are ready to serve the salad, toss the salad so that all the ingredients are well combined.

Salade Verte aux Herbes

Imagine walking through a herb garden and picking a few leaves from each of the plants as you stroll past them. If you cup your hands around the leaves, the aroma of the herbs — their oils perfuming the tips of your fingers — will be enchanting. The more herbs the better. The wonderful thing about this salad is that it's slightly different each time. If you don't grow your own herbs — no problem — try the selection listed below. If you have more of one than another, that's okay too. Do watch out for herbs that have a very strong aroma such as tarragon (a little goes a long way) or rosemary, which I would not recommend.

Serves 8 people

1/4 cup olive oil

1 tablespoon aged red wine vinegar or sherry vinegar

Zest of 1 lemon

Sea salt and black pepper to taste

12 oz mixed field greens — preferably with arugula in the mix

1 tablespoon dill — finely chopped

1 tablespoon fresh, small basil leaves — left whole

1 tablespoon fresh chives — finely chopped

1 tablespoon fresh Italian parsley — finely chopped

1 tablespoon fresh cilantro — stems removed, leaves left whole

1 Pour the olive oil and vinegar into a large salad bowl and whisk until the vinaigrette is homogeneous. Add the lemon zest, salt and pepper. Whisk again.

2 Place the serving utensils in the bowl over the vinaigrette. Place all the chopped herbs and the mixed greens on top of the utensils. Do not let any of the greens sit in the vinaigrette. The greens will wilt if they sit in the vinaigrette for any length of time. When you are ready to serve the salad, remove the serving utensils and toss the salad.

Note: People's taste in vinaigrettes vary considerably. This recipe can be made more or less strong by adding more or less vinegar. If too much olive oil is added, the vinaigrette will separate.

Salade Mesclun

Salade Mesclun is the epitome of the Provençal salad. The name is derived from the old Provençal word *mescal* — literally meaning "to mix." It originated in the area around Nice and is traditionally made up of leafy greens, chervil, arugula and endives. Now the mixture includes all sorts of other greens including frisée, dandelion greens and mache, to name a few. The salad is made from young shoots that are now often grown and harvested together.

It's usually served with lardons (thin matchstick-sized pieces of cooked bacon fat), and on occasion warm goat cheese or a poached egg. It's quite hard to find lardons outside of France, but bacon works just as well. I like to have a piece of warm baguette with this salad, and perhaps some soft goat cheese. The perfect lunch!

Serves 8 people

4 slices of bacon

2 tablespoons hazelnut oil or walnut oil

2 tablespoons olive oil

1/4 tablespoon Dijon mustard

1 tablespoon white wine vinegar

Sea salt and black pepper

12 oz mesclun salad greens

Freshly chopped chives

1   Place the slices of bacon in a small sauté pan over medium-high heat. Cook until they are crispy. Place the cooked bacon on paper towels to cool. Cut into small pieces.

2   Pour the oils into a large salad bowl and add the mustard. Stir well to combine. Then add the vinegar and a little salt and pepper and stir again. Place serving utensils over the vinaigrette and then place the salad greens, chives and bacon pieces on top of the utensils, making sure the salad does not fall into the vinaigrette.

3   When you are ready to serve, toss the salad gently so that everything is well combined.

Winter Greens Salad with Goat Cheese and Herbs

Winter food is so often full of soups and stews (which I adore by the way), but it's nice to freshen things up a bit with a salad like this one. It's a simple winter green salad to brighten up even the wettest and coldest of days.

Serves 8 people

1 tablespoon mustard

¼ cup olive oil

1 tablespoon red wine vinegar or fig balsamic vinegar

Sea salt and black pepper

12 oz mixed winter greens (if you can find pea greens add them to the mix too, and perhaps some watercress)

4-6 oz fresh, crumbled goat cheese

2 tablespoons parsley — finely chopped

2 tablespoons cilantro — finely chopped

1 tablespoon chives — finely chopped

1 Combine the mustard, olive oil and vinegar in the bottom of a large salad bowl and whisk together to form a thick emulsion. Add a little salt and pepper and whisk again. Place serving utensils over the vinaigrette and then place all the salad greens, herbs and goat cheese on top of the utensils.

2 When you are ready to serve the salad, toss it gently so that everything is well combined.

Mache Salad with a Pomegranate Vinaigrette

I had originally made this salad with orange Vincotto (literally "cooked wine"), a delicacy I had come across in a wonderful cheese shop in Los Angeles. Having run out and unable to find a replacement, I tried using pomegranate molasses, a semi-thick, sweet (but not in a cloying way) syrup made by cooking pomegranate juice and sugar. It is widely used in Middle Eastern cuisines and has a unique flavor, akin to a good balsamic and mashed-up fruit all in one. Adding white wine vinegar or Champagne vinegar to the vinaigrette lightens the mixture yet maintains the flavor and texture of the molasses. Be sure when you make the salad that the greens do not sit in the vinaigrette for too long as mache greens are quite delicate and will wilt.

Serves 8 people

3 tablespoons olive oil

2 teaspoons pomegranate molasses

1 teaspoon white wine vinegar

Large pinch grey sea salt

Freshly ground pepper

8 oz mache salad greens (also known as lamb's lettuce)

1 oz pomegranate seeds

1 Pour the olive oil into a large salad bowl. Add the molasses and vinegar, salt and 3–4 grinds of pepper. Whisk well to combine. Place salad utensils over the vinaigrette and then place the mache on top of the serving utensils so that the mache is not sitting in the vinaigrette.

2 When you are ready to serve the salad, toss it gently so that everything is well combined. Divide the salad evenly between the salad plates, and then sprinkle the pomegranate seeds on top.

Mache Salad with Bresaola and Goat Cheese

I first came across Bresaola — an air-cured, dried beef — while eating Raclette in the mountains near my grandparents' home in France. The hot melted cheese was poured across little steamed potatoes, served with assorted cured meats and an excellent, garlicky salad. It was the perfect dish to warm us up in the freezing weather.

This salad is a play on that dish. Bresaola is tender and salty, the goat cheese has a little tang to it and the mache is delicate and sweet. You can add some steamed, sliced fingerling potatoes if you like.

Serves 8 people

1 tablespoon basil oil

1 tablespoon balsamic
    vinegar

Coarse sea salt

Freshly ground black pepper

1 lb mache salad —
    cleaned and spun dry

½ cup salted pistachios —
    coarsely chopped

8 oz goat cheese —
    cold and crumbled

48 thin slices Bresaola or,
    if you prefer, Prosciutto
    (32 slices)

1 tablespoon chives —
    finely chopped

1   Pour the basil oil and the balsamic vinegar into a salad bowl. Add a good pinch of salt and 5–6 turns of black pepper. Whisk to combine. Toss in the mache, pistachios and goat cheese and toss again to coat.

2   Arrange the Bresaola slices on a large serving platter or divide equally between individual plates. Place the mache salad on top of the cured beef. Sprinkle the chives over the top.

Wilted Spinach Salad with Preserved Lemons

I admit to having a bit of an obsession with preserved lemons. I tend to go through phases where I obsess about a particular fruit, vegetable or spice. The preserved lemon phase is lasting a long time. This is one of the dishes I made when I had a plethora of lemons in the kitchen. The zing of the lemons with the golden raisins is delightful, and I know that although olives might sound odd in there, it's one of those salt-sweet-tangy marriages that works well.

Serves 8 people

3 tablespoons olive oil

1 1/2 lbs baby spinach — washed and dried

3 shallots — peeled and thinly sliced

Peel of 1/2 preserved lemon — finely chopped

1/2 cup assorted olives — pitted and chopped

1/4 cup golden raisins

Coarse sea salt

Black pepper

1 Pour 2 tablespoons olive oil into a large pan placed over medium-high heat. Add the baby spinach and cook until it is just wilted. This will only take a minute or so. Depending on the size of your pan, you may need to cook the spinach in batches. Transfer the wilted spinach to a large bowl.

2 In the same pan you just cooked the spinach, add 1 tablespoon olive oil and the shallots and cook for 2–3 minutes. Add the chopped preserved lemon, olives, golden raisins, a pinch of salt and 3–4 grinds of pepper. Cook, stirring frequently, for 2 minutes more. Pour this mixture over the spinach and toss to combine well. Serve at room temperature.

Arugula Salad with Shaved Pecorino and Caramelized Onions

I absolutely love caramelized onions. Maybe that's why a Tarte a l'Onion is one of my favorite dishes. This salad is akin to an onion tart without the tart shell. The onions cook slowly, become golden brown, soft and sweet. The shaved Pecorino (you can use other hard cheeses such as Manchego or Parmesan) adds a salty-nutty element that plays well with the pepperiness of the arugula. Try to serve it whilst the onions are still warm — it's even better that way!

Serves 8 people

Olive oil (for cooking the onions)

2–3 large yellow onions — peeled, halved and thinly sliced

1 teaspoon honey

1 teaspoon fresh thyme leaves

Coarse sea salt and pepper

1/3 cup olive oil

2 tablespoons fig balsamic vinegar

8 oz fresh arugula

1/2 bunch cilantro — finely chopped

4 oz Pecorino — use a cheese slicer to make thin shavings

1 Pour a little olive oil into a medium-sized skillet placed over medium-high heat. Add the sliced onions, honey and thyme leaves. Cook, stirring frequently, for 8–10 minutes. Reduce the heat, add some coarse sea salt and pepper and let the onions soften until golden brown. Set aside.

2 Pour the olive oil and vinegar into the bottom of a large salad bowl and whisk together. Place salad utensils over the vinaigrette and place the arugula and cilantro over the utensils. When you are ready to serve the salad, toss it gently so that the ingredients are well combined.

3 Divide the salad equally between eight plates. Spoon an equal amount of the caramelized onions on top of the arugula and cilantro mixture. Place some of the shaved Pecorino on top of the onions.

Fairview Gardens Arugula, Spinach and Dandelion Salad

A few years ago, on a blustery spring day, I was asked to teach a class at an urban farm. Fairview Gardens, a beautiful oasis located in the city of Goleta, is a 12.5 acre organic farm that grows everything from white asparagus to pomegranates. The Fairview staff asked me to prepare a menu from the garden's produce. This is the salad we made that day.

Time slowed down as we walked through the rows and rows of burgeoning vegetables, harvesting things we needed. If ever there was a moment to reconnect with nature, this was it. We prepared the food and ate outside on long trestle tables overlooking the garden. It was as though we were transported to an idyllic time when the hustle and bustle of the city did not press upon us.

Serves 8 people

Olive Oil

3 shallots — peeled and sliced

1 tablespoon red wine vinegar or sherry vinegar

Zest of 1 orange or other sweet citrus fruit such as tangerines or mandarins

Sea salt and black pepper to taste

2 tablespoons fresh parsley — finely chopped

1/2 bunch fresh chives — finely chopped

2 apples — sweet crunchy ones such as Gala or Fuji — cored, quartered and thinly sliced

4 oz pistachios — roughly chopped

4 oz dried cranberries or cherries

6 oz feta cheese — crumbled

1 lb altogether of fresh arugula, dandelion and spinach — cleaned and de-stemmed

1 Pour a little olive oil (about 1 tablespoon) into a small saucepan or skillet placed over medium heat. Add the shallots and cook for 5 minutes, stirring frequently. They should be a light golden brown color. Remove from the heat and add 1/4 cup olive oil, the vinegar, orange zest and some coarse salt and pepper. Whisk vigorously. Return to the stove and warm through.

2 Pour the warm vinaigrette into the bottom of a large salad bowl. Place serving utensils in the bowl over the vinaigrette. Place all the chopped herbs, apples, nuts, cranberries and feta on top of the utensils and cover them with the arugula, dandelion and spinach. When you are ready to serve the salad, toss the salad, making sure that the ingredients are well combined.

NOTE: This is excellent served with sun-dried tomato and olive crostini as a main course for lunch.

Spring Salad with Goat Cheese Crostini

I really like crostini — little toasts covered with delectable morsels, marinated mushrooms, olive tapenade, or in this case, simple goat cheese drizzled with a really rich wine-infused vinaigrette. Crostini are wonderful by themselves but can really enhance a salad and turn it into a mini meal.

Serves 8 people

For the vinaigrette:

⅓ cup red wine (such as a merlot or zinfandel)

⅓ cup balsamic vinegar

2 tablespoons golden raisins

3 tablespoons olive oil

Pinch of sea salt and black pepper

For the salad and crostini:

6 oz mixed salad greens — try to add some leaves that are a little peppery (such as arugula, dandelion or watercress)

16 small thin slices baguette or olive bread — toasted

4 oz goat cheese — crumbled

Golden raisins (from the recipe above)

Red wine and balsamic vinegar reduction (from the recipe above)

1 Place the red wine and balsamic vinegar in a small saucepan over low heat. Let the mixture reduce by two-thirds. This will take about 15–20 minutes. At the half-way stage, add the golden raisins, and make sure they are submerged. Stir the ingredients occasionally. Once the mixture has thickened, remove from the heat to cool.

2 Strain the golden raisins (I like to use a tea strainer for this), reserving the reduced liquid in a small bowl.

3 In a medium-sized salad bowl, whisk together 1 tablespoon of the red wine-vinegar reduction with the olive oil. Reserve the remaining reduction for the crostini. Stir in a pinch of salt and a touch of pepper. Place serving utensils over the vinaigrette.

4 Place the salad greens on top of the utensils and set aside.

5 Spread a little goat cheese on top of each slice of toast. Dot with a few golden raisins and drizzle a little of the reserved reduction over the cheese.

6 Toss the salad so that the ingredients are well combined and divide it equally between eight plates. Place a couple of the crostini on each plate alongside the salad.

Mustard Greens, Mint, Date and Manchego Salad

Many years ago, a good friend of mine introduced me to Barhi dates. They were a revelation. They taste rich, honey-filled and decadent. They are soft and luxurious on the inside. It's as though you're eating the most amazing piece of soft caramel and toffee all rolled into one. The down side of this variety is that the season is short. They keep for ages in the fridge, though.

I always buy a bag or two or three of them at the farmers' market, when they are in season. The trick is not eating them all before I get home. I have tried using these dates in all sorts of dishes from desserts (including shortbread — absolutely yummy) to various salads.

I came across some beautiful mustard greens at the market and thought about making a salad with them. Adding salted blistered almonds and Manchego to the mix creates a succulent-savory-salty melange. You can try this with different cheeses, too — sliced Pecorino or pieces of a dry-aged goat cheese work well.

The dates are rather addictive and versatile. I think I'll try a couscous with dates, caramelized onions and spices next.

Serves 8 people

1/3 cup good, fruity extra-virgin olive oil

1 tablespoon balsamic vinegar

1 teaspoon white wine vinegar

Pinch of coarse sea salt

Black pepper

10 oz mustard greens — washed and dried

1 large bunch mint — about 40–50 leaves

4 oz Manchego — very thinly sliced

2/3 cup blistered almonds — (or Marcona almonds) roughly chopped

1 cup dates — Barhi or soft Medjool if possible — pitted and chopped

1 Whisk the olive oil, vinegars, salt and black pepper together in a large salad bowl. Place the salad utensils on top of the vinaigrette and set aside.

2 Make sure all the mustard greens are clean and dry and place them on top of the salad utensils. Add the mint leaves, sliced Manchego, almonds and chopped dates to the bowl. When you are ready to serve the salad, let the greens fall gently into the vinaigrette and toss well to combine.

Kale and Spinach Salad with Honeyed Shallots and Plums

This salad came about during the photo shoot for this book. I had just picked the first plums of the season from my tree. They sat glistening on the counter top. They were juicy and sweet. I thought they would pair nicely with the roasted kale and made a test version of the salad. We liked it so much I never made the original salad planned for that day's photo session. The juice from the plums combines with the vinaigrette, creating a sweet counterpoint to the salty-crunchy texture of the kale and pecans. It's good with a little cheese, too — perhaps some feta, goat or a crumbled blue.

Serves 8 people

2 bunches kale — cleaned, stem ends trimmed and then cut into 1-inch wide strips

Olive oil

Sea salt and black pepper

12 shallots — peeled and quartered

1 tablespoon honey

10-12 plums — cut into eighths

1 tablespoon chives — finely chopped

3/4 cup pecan halves

1 tablespoon Dijon mustard

1/4 cup olive oil

1 tablespoon red wine vinegar

8 oz spinach

1 Preheat oven to 350 degrees.

2 Place the kale on a baking sheet and drizzle lightly with olive oil. Toss to coat. Sprinkle with some salt and pepper. Bake in the center of the oven for 8 minutes.

3 While the kale is roasting, pour a little olive oil into a cast-iron skillet or heavy-bottomed pan placed over medium heat. Add the shallots and cook for 5 minutes, turning occasionally. Add the honey and plums and cook for 5 minutes more. Add the chives and pecans, a little black pepper and toss the ingredients to combine. Remove from the heat.

4 Place the mustard in the bottom of a large salad bowl and whisk in 1/4 cup olive oil and the vinegar to form a smooth emulsion. It should look like a light mayonnaise. Add the shallot-plum mixture, the roasted kale and the spinach. Toss to combine all the ingredients well. Serve while the kale is still warm.

APPLE & PEARS

Apple Salad
with Fig Preserve and
Manchego Crostini

—

Apple, Pear and
Truffle Salad

—

Apple, Grape and
Walnut Salad

—

Salad with
Glazed Apples and
Goat Cheese

—

Pear and Fennel
Salad

—

Kale, Apple and
Almond Salad

—

Pear Carpaccio
with a Mache and
Roquefort Salad

Apple Salad with Fig Preserve and Manchego Crostini

When I was little, maybe five or six, my father once handed me a piece of toast with some honey and cheese on it. I was a little skeptical. Cheese and honey? "Just try it," he said. I took a tentative bite and discovered a delicious treat. I have been eating it ever since. I've tried different jams, preserves and flavors of honey with a variety of hard cheeses. One of my favorite combinations is fig preserve with nutty flavored Manchego. They work together well like apples and cheese.

Serves 8 people

1 tablespoon mustard

3 tablespoons olive oil

1 tablespoon fig balsamic
    vinegar

6 apples (different varieties
    if possible) — peeled and
    finely sliced

2 tablespoons pistachios —
    chopped

½ bunch chives —
    finely chopped

2 tablespoons basil leaves

8 slices olive bread

Basil olive oil

Fig preserve

Manchego cheese —
    thinly sliced

1 Combine the mustard, olive oil and vinegar in a medium-sized salad bowl and whisk to form a thick emulsion. Place salad utensils over the vinaigrette and place the apple slices, pistachios, chives and basil on top. When you are ready to serve the salad, toss all the ingredients together.

2 For the crostini, toast the bread and then drizzle with a little basil olive oil. Spread some of the fig preserve on the toast and then add the sliced Manchego cheese on top. Serve the crostini alongside the apple salad.

Apple, Pear and Truffle Salad

This salad is a little decadent. I like to think that being decadent once in awhile is good for you (and me, too). Anything with truffles in it fits the bill. You can use white or black truffles in this salad. Truffle shavings can be found in most gourmet delicatessens. They come in little jars, one of which is usually sufficient to make the salad for eight people.

Serves 8 people

For the vinaigrette:

All of the oil from the jar of shaved truffles (see below), plus enough olive oil to equal 3 tablespoons

1 tablespoon apple cider vinegar or white wine vinegar

Sea salt and black pepper

For the salad:

4 oz mache greens

3 oz goat cheese with truffles

4 pears — cored, peeled and thinly sliced

4 apples — cored, peeled and thinly sliced

1 small jar truffle shavings in olive oil

Black pepper

1/2 bunch flat-leafed parsley — finely chopped

1 Pour the truffle and olive oil mixture into the bottom of a large salad bowl. Add the vinegar and whisk to blend well. Add a pinch of salt and some black pepper. Place the salad utensils over the vinaigrette.

2 Place the mache greens and goat cheese on top of the serving utensils. When you are ready to serve the salad, toss it gently so that everything is well combined. Taste again for seasoning and adjust if necessary.

3 Arrange the apple and pear slices in an attractive pattern on each plate. Spoon some of the mache salad on top of the apples and pears. Spoon a little of the truffle shavings over each salad. Grind some black pepper over the greens and sprinkle a little parsley on top.

Apple, Grape and Walnut Salad

In 1893, the maître d'hôtel at The Waldorf Astoria created a salad that has become synonymous with that fine establishment. It was originally made with red apples, celery and grapes (walnuts were added later) all tossed in mayonnaise. I had a Waldorf Salad on my first trip to the United States (many years ago), and the memory of that salad has stayed with me. Mine is by no means a Waldorf salad; however, the apple-walnut combination does stem from that day. I like to add grapes to salads. They are sweet and juicy, and pair well with the blue cheese that is used in the vinaigrette.

This is a great salad for a picnic.

Serves 8 people

For the vinaigrette:

1 oz blue cheese — mashed

3 tablespoons olive oil

½ tablespoon Champagne vinegar or white wine vinegar

Sea salt and black pepper

Zest of 1 lemon

For the salad:

1 ½ lbs assorted grapes — halved

6 apples — cored, quartered and thinly sliced

½ cup pecans and walnuts — chopped

1 tablespoon chives — finely chopped

1 tablespoon parsley — finely chopped

1 Combine all the vinaigrette ingredients in the bottom of a large salad bowl. Whisk together well so that you have a homogeneous vinaigrette. Place serving utensils over the vinaigrette.

2 Add all the salad ingredients to the bowl, on top of the utensils. When you are ready to serve the salad, toss it gently so that everything is well combined.

NOTE: If you are taking this salad on a picnic, I would recommend putting the vinaigrette in a separate container, and then adding it to the salad bowl once you get to your destination. There is nothing worse than a soggy salad.

Salad with Glazed Apples and Goat Cheese

I love making salads with a warm ingredient in them, particularly when there is cheese. In this case, the warm ingredient is glazed apples. When you toss the salad, the cheese melts a little and mixes with the vinaigrette. It's really scrumptious.

Serves 8 people

4 Granny Smith apples —
  peeled, cored and thinly
  sliced

2 tablespoons butter

1 tablespoon light brown
  sugar

1 tablespoon Dijon mustard

3 tablespoons olive oil

1 tablespoon good, aged red
  wine vinegar or sherry
  vinegar

Sea salt and black pepper

6-8 oz mixed field greens —
  preferably with arugula in
  the mix

1 tablespoon fresh dill —
  finely chopped

1 tablespoon fresh basil —
  finely chopped

1 tablespoon fresh chives —
  finely chopped

1 tablespoon fresh Italian
  parsley — finely chopped

5 oz goat cheese

1 Melt the butter in a large skillet placed over medium heat. When the butter foams, toss in the apple slices and sauté until golden brown. Sprinkle the sugar over the apples and cook for a few more minutes until the sugar and butter become syrupy and almost caramelized. Remove the pan from the heat, leaving the apples in the pan until you are ready to assemble the salad.

2 Place one rounded tablespoon of mustard in the bottom of a salad bowl. Slowly drizzle in the olive oil and whisk just until the vinaigrette resembles the consistency of a light mayonnaise. If too much olive oil is added, the vinaigrette will separate. Add the vinegar and whisk until the vinaigrette is homogeneous. Add a pinch of salt and pepper to taste.

3 Place the serving utensils in the bowl over the vinaigrette, then place all the chopped herbs and mixed greens on top of the utensils. Do not let any of the greens sit in the vinaigrette.

4 Crumble the goat cheese into the bowl and add the glazed apples. When you are ready to serve the salad, toss it gently so that everything is well combined.

Pear and Fennel Salad

Pears and fennel are one of those perfect pairings. They complement each other as the anise taste of the crunchy fennel combines with the soft, sweet and slightly grainy pears. Try to find pears that are a little juicy but not overly ripe so that they will hold their shape in the salad. This salad has layers of flavors that mingle with each other in such a way that no two mouthfuls taste exactly alike.

Serves 8 people

4 tablespoons olive oil

3 shallots — peeled, halved and thinly sliced

1 tablespoon aged red wine vinegar or sherry vinegar

Zest of 1 lemon

Sea salt and black pepper

2 oz fresh cilantro — leaves only

1 bunch fresh chives — finely chopped

4 pears — cored, quartered and thinly sliced

2 large fennel bulbs — quartered and thinly sliced

4 oz pistachios or almonds or a mixture of both — roughly chopped

4 oz feta cheese

4 oz fresh arugula

4 oz fresh mixed greens

1. Pour 1 tablespoon of olive oil into a small skillet placed over medium heat. Add the shallots and cook for 5 minutes, stirring frequently. They should be a light golden brown color. Remove the pan from the heat and add the 3 remaining tablespoons of olive oil, the vinegar, lemon zest, a pinch of coarse salt and pepper. Whisk vigorously. Return to the stove for 1–2 minutes.

2. Pour the warm vinaigrette into the bottom of a large salad bowl. Place the serving utensils in the bowl over the vinaigrette. Then place all the chopped herbs, pears, fennel, nuts and feta on top of the utensils. Cover this with the arugula and mixed greens. When you are ready to serve the salad, toss it gently so that everything is well combined.

Kale, Apple and Almond Salad

Kale salads are all the rage right now (well, kale in general). It's become THE hot green, if that's possible. I think that spinach had its glory days some years ago, and then it was arugula's turn. The thing is, I LOVE kale. It's a vegetable I discovered relatively recently. We did not eat kale in London where I grew up. Spinach, yes. Chard, check. Arugula, absolutely. Kale, not a mouthful — until I came to California. Now I add it to everything. It has become another one of my fads, although I think that this one will never fade. I have made tons of kale dishes — roasted kale, crispy kale chips, raw kale salad — well, you get the general idea. Here's one of my favorites.

Serves 8 people

For the vinaigrette:

4 tablespoons olive oil

Juice of 1/2 lemon

2 tablespoons chives — finely chopped

1 tablespoon parsley — finely chopped

1 rounded tablespoon Greek yogurt

Sea salt and black pepper

For the salad:

2 bunches kale — rinsed and chopped

Olive oil

Sea salt and black pepper

Juice of 1 lemon

4-5 apples — cored, quartered and then thinly sliced

1/4 lb almonds — roughly chopped

1 Preheat the oven to 350 degrees.

2 Place all the vinaigrette ingredients in a large salad bowl and whisk together well. Place salad utensils over the vinaigrette.

3 Place the chopped kale on a baking sheet or in a roasting pan. Drizzle with olive oil and toss to coat evenly. Sprinkle with coarse salt and freshly ground black pepper. Roast for 7–8 minutes. The kale will be just wilted and bits of it will be slightly crunchy. As soon as you take the kale out of the oven, pour the lemon juice over it and toss gently.

4 Add the cooked kale and the remaining salad ingredients to the bowl and toss well. This is one salad that actually benefits from being tossed at least 10 minutes before you serve it.

Pear Carpaccio with a Mache and Roquefort Salad

Traditionally, carpaccio is a dish of paper-thin beef or fish that is drizzled with olive oil or lemon juice. In this dish, it's the pears that have been thinly sliced to create the carpaccio. The pears are sliced horizontally to create round disks. You can slice them lengthwise and fan out the pears, if you prefer.

Serves 8 people

3 tablespoons lemon
olive oil

1 tablespoon Champagne
vinegar

Sea salt and black pepper

4 oz mache

2 oz Roquefort cheese —
crumbled

1 bunch chives — finely
chopped

1 tablespoon pecans —
chopped

1 tablespoon pistachios —
chopped

4 Asian pears — peeled
and sliced horizontally to
create 1/8-inch disks

1 lemon — halved

1 Mix together the olive oil and vinegar in the bottom of a large salad bowl. Add a pinch of salt and some freshly ground black pepper. Place salad utensils over the vinaigrette.

2 Place the mache, Roquefort, chives and nuts on top of the serving utensils and set aside until ready to serve.

3 Arrange the very thinly sliced pear disks in a circular pattern on each salad plate, covering the central part of each plate completely. Squeeze some lemon juice over the pears.

4 Toss the salad and divide it equally between the plates, placing the salad on top of the pears.

ASPARAGUS

Warm Asparagus
and Smoked Salmon

—

Roasted Purple
Asparagus with
Baby Kale

—

Asparagus Trio
Salad with Arugula
and Basil

—

White Asparagus
Salad with Olives
and Herb Pesto
Vinaigrette

—

Asparagus, Salmon
and Herb Verrines

—

Grilled Asparagus
and Snap Pea Salad

Warm Asparagus and Smoked Salmon

This is a dish I first made as a teenager in London. It's very simple and easy to make. It multiplies easily and works well for large dinner parties or a buffet. You can use white asparagus or mix varieties, as all types of asparagus and smoked salmon are terrific together.

Serves 8 people

2 1/2 lbs asparagus (choose stalks that are not too thick) about 9 spears per person — ends trimmed

1/2 lb smoked salmon — thinly sliced

1 tablespoon Dijon mustard

1/4 cup olive oil

1 tablespoon white wine vinegar or Champagne vinegar

1 tablespoon chives — finely chopped

Large pinch of flake salt (Murray River Salt or Maldon Salt work well)

Black pepper

1 Cook the asparagus in a steamer until they are al dente. This should take about 5 minutes. Remove from the steamer and place them in a shallow dish filled with iced water to stop the cooking and keep the asparagus bright green.

2 Remove the asparagus from the ice water and pat dry.

3 Assemble bundles of asparagus by wrapping 1/2 slice of smoked salmon around 3 spears. Arrange 3 bundles on each salad plate.

4 To make the vinaigrette, combine the mustard, olive oil and vinegar in a small bowl and whisk together to create a homogeneous sauce. Drizzle the vinaigrette over the salmon-wrapped asparagus and then sprinkle some chives over each serving. Add a pinch of salt and some black pepper.

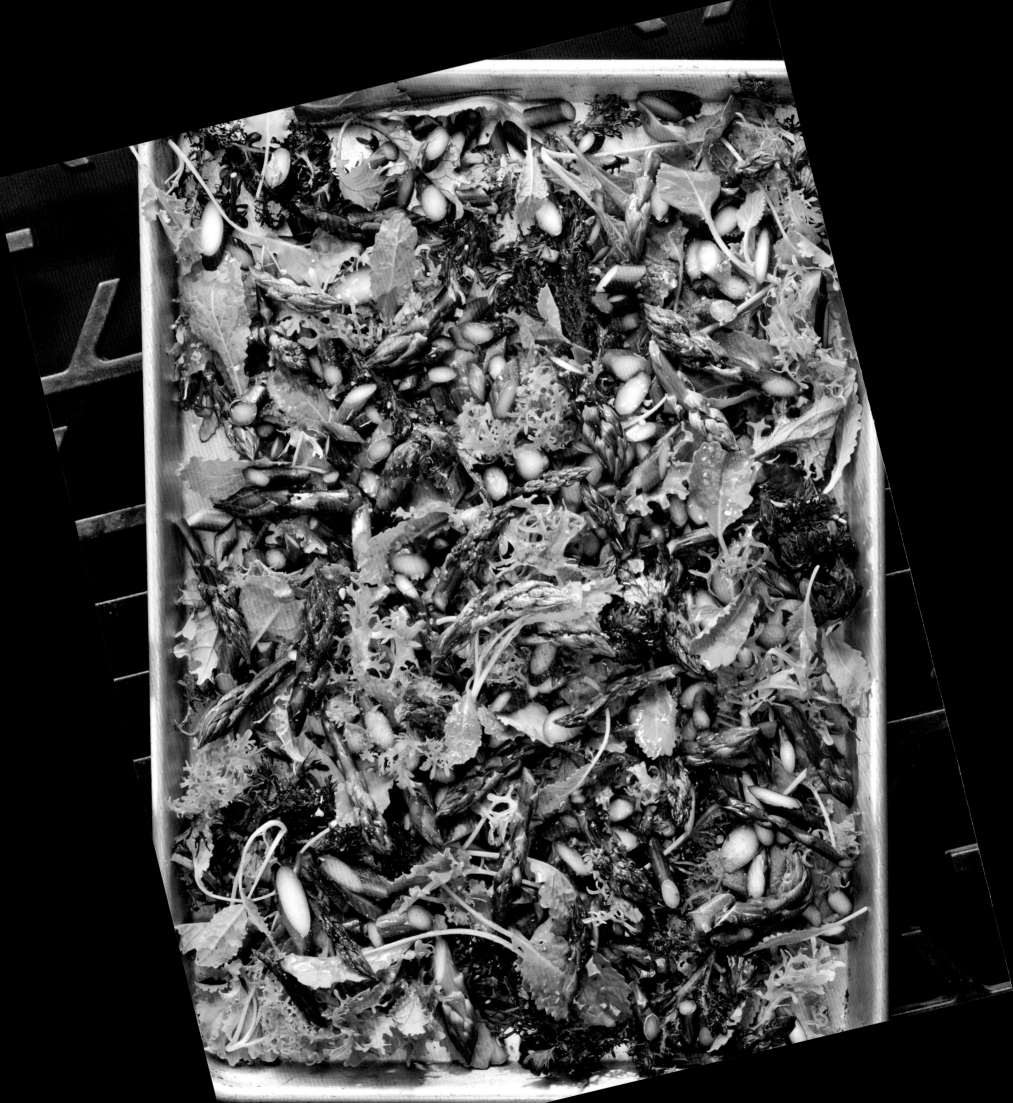

Roasted Purple Asparagus with Baby Kale

This salad combines two of my favorite ingredients: asparagus and kale. The purple asparagus adds color and has a slightly more bitter taste than the green variety, which can of course be substituted here if you cannot find the purple. This is an easy salad to make and is wonderful on busy weekday evenings as it takes just minutes to prepare. You can add all sorts of things to this. I just made a variation that had green onions, cherry tomatoes and almonds to bring to my book club potluck. These evenings have turned into monthly major vegetarian feasts. A good book to discuss, good friends and good food — what could be better than that?

Serves 8 people

For the salad:

1 large bunch baby kale — chopped

1 bunch mustard greens — chopped

1 bunch pea tendrils — chopped

2 lbs purple asparagus — tips trimmed and the rest of the stalk cut on a bias into 1/2-inch pieces

Olive oil

Sea salt and black pepper

For the vinaigrette:

4 tablespoons olive oil

Juice and zest of 1 lemon

1 tablespoon Champagne vinegar

1 teaspoon fig balsamic vinegar or other fruity balsamic vinegar

40–50 Thai basil leaves

30–40 green basil leaves

1. Preheat the oven to 350 degrees.

2. Place the chopped kale, mustard greens and pea tendrils on a baking sheet or in a shallow roasting pan. Scatter the chopped asparagus over the top of the greens. Drizzle a little olive oil over the vegetables, just to coat. Add a pinch of salt and grind some pepper over the entire dish.

3. Pop the dish in the oven for 7 minutes, turning the vegetables once during the cooking time.

4. While the vegetables are cooking, prepare the vinaigrette. Combine the olive oil with the lemon juice, lemon zest and vinegars in a large salad bowl and whisk together vigorously to make a homogeneous vinaigrette. Add all the greens and the two types of basil and toss well. Serve while the salad is still warm.

Asparagus Trio Salad with Arugula and Basil

This is one of those dishes that was inspired by a walk through the farmers' market. It was in the middle of asparagus season with fresh green stalks piled up everywhere. When I came across some purple asparagus, they were so beautiful to look at, I couldn't resist them. The stalks are a deep burgundy with flashes of green peeking through. The same day, I found some white asparagus in another market. The trio of colors looked so appetizing on my kitchen counter that I decided to make a salad with all three. By a complete coincidence, I had three varieties of basil in my garden and used the small tender leaves from each in the salad. Thai basil is quite strong, so I wouldn't use too much of it, as it may overpower the delicate flavors of the asparagus.

Serves 8 people

Juice and zest of 1 large lemon

5 tablespoons olive oil

Sea salt and black pepper

4 oz arugula

1 small bunch of each green, purple and Thai basil — leaves removed from the stems and left whole

½ lb each green, white and purple asparagus — tips trimmed and left whole, the rest of the stalk cut on a bias into very thin slices

½ lb English peas — shelled (that is the shelled weight so you'll need about 2 lbs with the shells on)

1 Pour the lemon juice, 4 tablespoons of olive oil, a pinch of salt and 4–5 grinds of pepper into the bottom of a medium-sized salad bowl. Whisk together well. Place salad utensils over the top of the vinaigrette. Place the arugula and basil leaves on top of the utensils and set aside.

2 Pour the remaining 1 tablespoon of olive oil into a large skillet placed over medium-high heat. Add the sliced asparagus, the asparagus tips, peas and lemon zest and sauté for 3–4 minutes, stirring occasionally. Remove from the heat.

3 Add the asparagus-pea mixture to the salad bowl. Toss all the ingredients until well combined. Divide the salad equally between the plates, The salad is lovely when the asparagus are still warm.

White Asparagus Salad with Olives and Herb Pesto Vinaigrette

I really became enamored of white asparagus on a trip to Austria many years ago. Everywhere we went, white asparagus were on the menu. They were beautiful, fat, juicy asparagus filled with a herbaceous, crisp flavor. Finding white asparagus that are as good as those has become an annual quest. Every now and then I'll come across a really good batch, and this is the salad I make with them.

Serves 8 people

2 lbs. white asparagus — stalks peeled and ends trimmed

3-4 tablespoons black Niçoise olives — pitted and chopped

1 small bunch chives — chopped

For the pesto vinaigrette:

1/4 cup olive oil

1/2 bunch cilantro (about 1 cup) — roughly chopped

1/2 bunch basil — roughly chopped

1 tablespoon parsley — roughly chopped

Juice and zest of 1 lemon

Juice and zest of 1 lime

Sea salt

Black pepper

1 Steam the asparagus for 8-9 minutes. They should be al dente. The white variety takes a little longer to cook than the green, but do take care not to overcook them. As soon as they are cooked, carefully remove the asparagus from the steamer and set aside to cool.

2 While the asparagus are cooking, purée all the pesto ingredients (except the lemon zest) in a blender until you have a green vinaigrette. Check the seasoning, adding more lemon juice, if needed. Pour the herb vinaigrette onto a serving platter so that it covers the bottom of the dish completely.

3 Place the asparagus on top of the vinaigrette and sprinkle them with the chopped olives and lemon zest. Grind a little black pepper over the top and serve immediately.

Asparagus, Salmon and Herb Verrines

There is something quite tantalizing about being able to see a dish in its entirety before you delve into it. Usually we look down on our food. The few exceptions are normally reserved for desserts. Ice cream sundaes and other cold desserts come to mind — usually served with one of those long skinny spoons to scoop out all the best bits that have sunk to the bottom. In these verrines, you get the same thing in a savory form.

The inspiration for this dish came from two sources. The first was a book on verrines that I found tucked away on a shelf in my father's house in Provence. I wish I had that book today, for it was chock-full of glass-filled delights. I had the memory of one of the photographs from it when, to my amazement, I came across another version of the smoked salmon and fingerling potatoes salad in Beatrice Peltre's excellent book, *La Tartine Gourmande.* This is my version, made with both salmon filet and smoked salmon, and with some crème fraiche in the yogurt mixture, a touch I know my grandmother from Normandy would have appreciated.

Serves 8 people

1/4 lb small purple potatoes

1/2 lb asparagus — reserving 16 tips for the garnish

1/2 lb haricots verts

2 cups Greek yogurt

2 tablespoons crème fraiche

Zest and juice of 2 lemons

1/2 bunch chives — finely chopped — reserving 1 tablespoon and 16 tips for garnish

2 tablespoons dill — finely chopped

2 tablespoons olive oil

Pinch of sea salt

4–5 grinds of black pepper

8 oz cooked salmon filet or smoked filet of salmon — flaked

8 oz smoked salmon — chopped

1 lemon — quartered

4 oz golden fish roe for garnish

8 sprigs dill (optional)

1 Steam the potatoes until just tender. Let cool and then thinly slice.

2 Steam the asparagus and haricots verts until just al dente. Remove from the steamer and set aside to cool. Both vegetables will need to be trimmed to fit inside the verrines. Slice the haricots verts in half, and the asparagus either in thirds or quarters so that they will fit inside your verrines.

3 Combine the yogurt, crème fraiche, lemon juice and zest, chives, dill and olive oil in a bowl and whisk together well. Add the pepper and a pinch of salt and mix again.

4 Spoon a little of the yogurt mixture into the bottom of each verrine. Lay the haricots verts halves horizontally on top of the yogurt. Divide the salmon filet equally between the verrines, placing it on top of the haricots verts.

5 Spoon a little more of the yogurt mixture over the salmon filet, then top this with the asparagus pieces. Cover the asparagus with remaining yogurt mixture.

6 Arrange the thinly sliced potatoes over the yogurt mixture in each verrine. Layer the smoked salmon over the sliced potatoes.

7 Squeeze a little fresh lemon juice over the salmon just before serving. Garnish with a sprig of dill or chives, the reserved asparagus tips and golden fish roe.

Grilled Asparagus and Snap Pea Salad

I have one of those cast-iron griddle pans that you can put on top of your stove. I never used it very much until about two years ago. I really wanted to grill something but didn't want to schlep and then clean my barbecue that was sitting outside under a tree, so I thought I'd give this griddle thing a try. Why did I not do this before? It's fantastic. I grill vegetables all the time now and add them to lots of salads. There are quite a few salads with grilled vegetables in this book. Asparagus cooked on the grill somehow tastes even better. I really like the little charred bits on the stalks that are earthy tasting. The salad makes me think of a spring garden with burgeoning vegetables.

Serves 8 people

1 tablespoon mustard

4 tablespoons olive oil

1 tablespoon red wine vinegar

Sea salt and black pepper

2 lbs asparagus

1 lb snap peas

1 small bunch chives — finely chopped

1 bunch basil leaves

1 small bunch fresh mint — leaves left whole if the leaves are small, otherwise roughly chopped

2 tablespoons pistachios

1 Combine the mustard, olive oil and vinegar in the bottom of a large salad bowl. Whisk until the emulsion resembles a light mayonnaise. Add a pinch of salt and some black pepper. Place serving utensils over the vinaigrette.

2 Pour a little olive oil into a large shallow dish. Place the asparagus and snap peas in the dish, sprinkle a little salt on them and shake the pan a few times to coat the vegetables.

3 Place a cast-iron griddle on the stove over medium-high heat. Once it is hot, lay the asparagus stalks and snap peas on the griddle and cook for 1 1/2 minutes. Turn once and cook for another minute. The vegetables should still be bright green and al dente. Carefully remove the cooked vegetables and place them on a cutting board. Slice the asparagus and snap peas on a bias, and then transfer them to the salad bowl.

4 Just before serving, add the chives, basil and mint leaves and pistachios to the bowl, and toss to combine the ingredients well.

BEETS

Roasted Red Beet,
Orange and Black
Olive Salad

~

Golden Beet and
Green Tomato Salad

~

Curry Roasted Golden
Beet Salad

~

Pascale's Birthday
Beet Salad

~

Chioggia and Red
Beet Salad

~

Warm Dandelion
and Watercress
Salad with Roasted
Root Vegetables,
Bacon and Herbs

Roasted Red Beet, Orange and Black Olive Salad

My appreciation of beets has come a long way. My first introduction to beets was as an unsuspecting schoolchild in London. They were inflicted on my classmates and me by a kitchen staff who must have taken a perverse pleasure in seeing us try to consume these gelatinous horrors. You can imagine, therefore, that I was not very keen to try beets again.

Many years later, now living in California, I came across some roasted golden beets in a salad at a restaurant in Los Angeles. These were a revelation. First of all, they were a little crunchy and had flavor that was nothing like the brine-soaked beets of my childhood. I was smitten and have been cooking with them, in a variety of guises, ever since.

This salad is a little exotic in a juicy way. Oranges and beets are great partners. The natural sugars in each play off each other; the lemon zest and onion add a spicy acidic note; and the cilantro is fresh and invigorating. This is one of my favorites.

Serves 8 people

4 tablespoons olive oil

4-6 red beets — peeled and cut into eighths

2 red onions — peeled and thinly sliced

Fig balsamic vinegar

Sea salt and black pepper

4 oranges — peeled and sectioned

1/2 cup black olives — pitted

1/2 bunch cilantro leaves

Zest of 1 lemon

1 Preheat the oven to 350 degrees.

2 Pour a little olive oil into an oven-proof dish. Place the beets and onions into the dish. Pour 1 tablespoon of fig balsamic over them. Sprinkle with salt and pepper and then toss to coat well.

3 Roast the beets and onions, covered, for 45 minutes to 1 hour, stirring the mixture once or twice. (You should be able to cut them in half easily, but they should not be too soft.) Let cool for 10 minutes.

4 While the beets are roasting, prepare the remaining salad ingredients. Pour 3 tablespoons of olive oil into the bottom of a salad bowl. Whisk in one tablespoon of the fig balsamic, the lemon zest, a pinch of salt and pepper. Place salad utensils on top of the vinaigrette.

5 Place the sectioned oranges, olives and cilantro leaves on top of the serving utensils. When the beets-onion mixture has cooled, add it to the salad bowl.

6 When you are ready to serve, toss all the ingredients together.

Golden Beet and Green Tomato Salad

Golden beets live up to their name. Sunflower yellow inside, they can transform a dish with a pop of color, and their natural sugars are enhanced when cooked. I couldn't resist the color combination of the golden beets and green tomatoes, hence, this salad.

Serves 8 people

For the salad:

8 medium-sized golden beets — peeled and thinly sliced on a mandolin

Olive oil

1 teaspoon white wine vinegar or pear Champagne vinegar

8 medium-sized green tomatoes — thinly sliced

1/2 bunch chives — finely chopped

1 bunch basil leaves

Sea salt

For the vinaigrette:

4 tablespoons olive oil

Juice of 1 lemon

Pinch of coarse sea salt

4–5 turns of black pepper

1. Pour a little olive oil into a large skillet placed over medium heat. Place the beet slices in the pan so that they barely overlap (you will probably need to do this in 2 or 3 batches). Drizzle a little of the white wine vinegar over the top, add a pinch of salt and cook for 3–4 minutes, turning the beets once or twice. The beets should be just cooked through. Remove the pan from the heat, leaving the beets in the pan. Cover and let rest for 3–4 minutes.

2. Arrange the beet slices in concentric circles on each plate. Insert a green tomato slice in-between every 3–4 beet slices.

3. Whisk all the vinaigrette ingredients together so that you have a smooth emulsion. Pour the vinaigrette over the beets and tomatoes, then sprinkle with the chopped chives. Insert the basil leaves in-between the beet and tomato slices.

Curry Roasted Golden Beet Salad

I once ate a chicken curry in London that brought tears to my eyes. It was so, so, so spicy, I couldn't eat enough yogurt to squelch the burning sensation in my throat. The person who cooked the curry made his own blend of curry powder (a mixture, which interestingly enough, doesn't really exist in India — curry being a type of food, not an actual spice). He evidently had a heavy hand when it came to hot spices.

Most curry powder recipes include coriander, turmeric, cumin, fenugreek and red pepper, with the possible addition of cardamom, cinnamon, cloves, mustard seeds and ginger. There are huge variations in curry blends. I like to make one that has less heat (I admit that I am a bit of a wimp when it comes to really spicy food). The idea, for me, is to create a dish that has a soupçon of those fragrant flavors but not one that is overpowered by them. This salad is one of those dishes. Beets and curry are delicious together as the spices enrich the sweet earthiness of the beets.

Serves 8 people

Olive oil

4–6 golden beets — cleaned and roots trimmed

Sea salt

6–8 shallots — peeled and quartered

6 oz golden raisins

2 teaspoons of your favorite curry powder

½ bunch cilantro leaves — left whole

4 oz feta cheese — crumbled (optional)

For the citrus vinaigrette:

4 tablespoons olive oil

Zest and juice of 1 orange

Zest and juice of 2 lemons

1 teaspoon white wine vinegar

Pinch of sea salt

3–4 grinds of black pepper

1 Preheat the oven to 350 degrees.

2 Place the golden beets on a sheet of foil that is large enough to envelop them. If the beets are very large, you may need to do this in 2 pouches. Drizzle a little olive oil over the beets and sprinkle with some coarse salt. Wrap them completely in the foil. Place the foil pouch(es) on a baking sheet and cook for 30 minutes. The beets should be relatively easy to pierce, but not too soft.

3 While the beets are roasting, prepare the remaining salad ingredients. Pour the vinaigrette ingredients into the bottom of a salad bowl and whisk together well. Place the salad utensils on top of the vinaigrette.

4 Pour a little olive oil into a medium-sized skillet placed over medium heat. Add the shallots, golden raisins and curry powder. Cook for 8–10 minutes or until the shallots are soft and golden. Place the raisin and shallot mixture and the cilantro leaves in the salad bowl.

5 Once the beets are cooked, remove from the oven and foil. Let rest for 10 minutes or until cool enough to handle. Peel the beets and cut them into thin wedges or slices and then add them to the salad bowl.

6 Toss all the ingredients together and let rest 10 minutes before serving. Serve while the beets are still warm. You can also add feta cheese to this salad, which melts a little with the warm beets.

Pascale's Birthday Beet Salad

Last year I celebrated my birthday by having a huge picnic in the middle of a vineyard. It was one of those perfect, sunny, warm spring days. We set up long trestle tables under large oak trees surrounded by acres of vines as far as the eye could see. The tables were laden with salads, cheese, fresh bread, salmon and fruit. This was one of the salads I made that morning. I had originally planned to make a straight beet salad. However, when I realized how many people we were going to be, I kept adding ingredients, and this is the salad it turned into.

Serves 8 to 10 people

6 golden beets

Olive oil

Coarse sea salt

2 long leeks — roots trimmed away, halved and thinly sliced

1 large yellow onion — peeled, halved and thinly sliced

6-8 shallots — peeled and sliced

3 tablespoons golden raisins

1 bunch green onions — root ends trimmed away and then finely chopped

Sea salt and black pepper

1 lb snap peas — trimmed and thinly sliced on a bias

1 lb English peas (1 lb shelled, so you will need at least twice that weight to net 1 lb)

8 oz baby spinach

1 bunch chives — finely chopped

Juice of 2-3 lemons

1 Preheat the oven to 350 degrees.

2 Place the golden beets on a sheet of foil that is large enough to envelop them. If the beets are very large you may need to do this in 2 pouches. Drizzle a little olive oil over the beets and sprinkle with some coarse salt. Wrap them completely in the foil. Place the foil pouch(es) on a baking sheet and cook for 30 minutes. Once the beets are cooked, remove from the oven and foil, and let cool for 10 minutes, or until cool enough to handle. Peel and cut them into thin wedges or slices.

3 Place the leeks, onions, shallots, golden raisins and green onions in a roasting pan and drizzle with some olive oil, a good pinch of salt and some pepper. Roast in the oven for 20 minutes, turning the mixture once or twice. Add the cooked beets to the roasting pan and cook for another 5 minutes.

4 Pour a little olive oil into a separate pan placed over medium heat. Add the snap peas, English peas, spinach and chives and cook for 3-4 minutes or until the spinach has wilted.

5 Place all of the vegetables from the oven and the pan into a salad bowl, toss to combine. Add some lemon juice and a drizzle of olive oil. Salt and pepper to taste, toss once more, *et voila!*

Chioggia and Red Beet Salad

Chioggia beets are one of nature's gems. When you cut them open, they reveal white and pink striations, a natural candy stripe. They are really quite beautiful. These markings tend to fade a little when you roast the beets but they will retain their coloring and will turn any salad into an edible painting.

Serves 8 people

For the salad:

4 chioggia beets

4 red beets

Olive oil

Sea salt

4 oz baby arugula

1/2 lb red seedless grapes — halved

1 bunch purple basil leaves

3 oz feta cheese

For the vinaigrette:

1 tablespoon Dijon mustard

4 tablespoons olive oil

1 tablespoon red wine vinegar

1. Preheat the oven to 350 degrees.

2. Place the beets on a sheet of foil that is large enough to envelop them. If the beets are very large, you may need to do this in 2 pouches. Drizzle a little olive oil over the beets and sprinkle with some coarse salt. Wrap them completely in the foil. Place the foil pouch(es) on a baking sheet and cook for 30 minutes.

3. Once the beets are cooked, remove them from the oven and the foil. Let rest until cool enough to handle. Peel and slice the beets as thin as possible. Use a mandolin if you have one.

4. Whisk the vinaigrette ingredients together in the bottom of a large salad bowl. Place serving utensils on top of the vinaigrette. Place the beet slices and remaining salad ingredients on top of the utensils. When you are ready to serve the salad, toss it gently so that everything is well combined.

Warm Dandelion and Watercress Salad with Roasted Root Vegetables, Bacon and Herbs

This salad came about as a result of a *Tour de Frigidaire,* or TDF as my friend Michele would say. It's a great expression that means making something out of all the bits that are left in your fridge. The first time I made this, there were three of us having an impromptu lunch. Here's the recipe for eight. Feel free to add other bits and pieces (goat cheese or feta would be great, for example) from your own *frigidaire*!

Serves 8 people

Olive oil

1 lb multi-colored carrots — peeled and cut into 2-inch pieces

1 large parsnip — peeled and chopped into long strips

2 lbs beets — golden, ruby or red — peeled and cut into quarters

4 slices of bacon — cut crosswise into thin strips

2 sprigs of fresh rosemary leaves

Sea salt and black pepper

1 tablespoon fig balsamic vinegar

8 oz dandelion greens — cleaned and roughly chopped

8 oz watercress — cleaned and roughly chopped

1/2 bunch dill — finely chopped

1/2 bunch parsley — finely chopped

1/2 bunch basil leaves — rolled up and thinly sliced

1 Preheat the oven to 350 degrees.

2 Pour a little olive oil onto a baking sheet and add the carrots, parsnips, beets, bacon strips, fresh rosemary and some salt and pepper. Toss to coat well. Roast in the oven for 45 minutes until tender. Stir the vegetables once or twice while they are cooking.

3 Pour a 1/4 cup olive oil into a salad bowl. Whisk in the fig balsamic vinegar, add a pinch of salt and some pepper. Place salad utensils over the vinaigrette. Place the dandelion and watercress on top of the utensils.

4 When you are ready to serve the salad, add all the roasted vegetables to the salad bowl and all of the remaining chopped herbs. Toss until well combined.

CARROTS

Classic French Bistro
Carrot Salad

~

Moroccan Carrot
Salad with Golden
Raisins

~

Roasted Kale and
Rainbow Carrot
Salad

~

Roasted Carrots,
Parsnips, Zucchini
and Onion Salad

~

Carrot, Radish and
Orange Salad

Classic French Bistro Carrot Salad

This is the simplest of salads. Carrots, lemon juice and olive oil. It's a classic salad in France that all small children eat. My grandmother made this salad for my brother and me all the time. Every time I eat this, it reminds me of her and of sitting in her kitchen on my favorite stool — the red one my brother and I used to fight over. We had to take turns sitting on it. We loved sitting in that kitchen eating all my grandmother's treats. This carrot salad was one of them.

Serves 8 people

2 lbs fresh carrots —
    peeled and coarsely
    grated

Juice and zest of 2–3 lemons

3 tablespoons olive oil

2 tablespoons parsley —
    finely chopped

Sea salt and black pepper

1 Place the carrots in a large salad bowl. Drizzle the olive oil and lemon juice over the carrots. Sprinkle the parsley over the carrots and add a pinch of salt and some pepper. Toss well to combine at least 10 minutes before serving.

Moroccan Carrot Salad with Golden Raisins

Morocco is known for its scented, flavorful cuisine, for its judicious use of spices and the layering of flavors within each dish. This carrot salad was inspired by some sweet, yellow carrots I found at the market along with some golden flame raisins. The raisins were huge, almost honey filled. We munched on them as we walked around the market picking up some of the other ingredients for dinner. I served this with a roasted chicken that had been cooked with Ras al Hanout and preserved lemons.

Serves 8 people

Olive oil

10-12 yellow carrots — peeled and thinly sliced

6 shallots — peeled, halved and thinly sliced

2 tablespoons golden raisins

1 pinch saffron threads

1 pinch cumin powder

Coarse sea salt and black pepper

Lemon olive oil

Zest of 1 lemon

1 small bunch cilantro leaves

2 tablespoons chives — finely chopped

1 Pour a little olive oil into a large pan placed over medium heat. Toss the carrots, shallots and golden raisins in the pan and coat with the oil. Sprinkle in the saffron and cumin and stir all the ingredients together. Cook for 8–10 minutes stirring frequently. The shallots should be soft and translucent, just barely cooked, and the saffron should be just releasing its fragrance.

2 Transfer the carrot-shallot mixture to a salad bowl. Drizzle with a little lemon olive oil, add a dash of salt and some black pepper, the lemon zest, chives and the cilantro leaves. Toss well to combine. I like serving this in small individual tagines, alongside a main course or as part of a series of small plates, tapas style.

Roasted Kale and Rainbow Carrot Salad

This salad is from a spring blog post of mine. I came across some sensational-looking rainbow carrots at the market and have been trying out all sorts of dishes with them. I've steamed them, roasted them, grated and chopped them. I love their color and really wanted to retain that in the finished dish. I found that if you cook the carrots for a short amount of time, they still retain some of their crunchiness and are visually very appetizing. Combine that with the earthy overtones of roasted kale, and you have the makings of a beautiful and very healthy salad. The great thing about this dish is that you can use any kind of kale. In fact, it's all the more appealing if you can find some purple kale and combine it with one of the curly green varieties. Kale is really easy to cook. All this salad needs is 10 minutes in the oven, and it's done. This salad can be prepped hours in advance and then popped into the oven at the last minute. I asked my kids to help prepare the carrots; they loved making the carrot ribbons.

Serves 8 people

2 lbs rainbow carrots — washed

2 lbs kale — different types — roughly chopped

Olive oil to drizzle, plus 1/4 cup olive oil

1 tablespoon fig balsamic vinegar

Zest and juice of 1 orange

Pinch of sumac

Sea salt and black pepper

1 Preheat the oven to 350 degrees.

2 Using a vegetable peeler, peel the carrots into thin shavings. Place the carrot shavings and the kale into a large bowl and drizzle with a little olive oil. Toss to coat well and then mound all the vegetables onto one sheet pan. They will be piled high — which is okay.

3 Roast the vegetables for 10 minutes.

4 While the vegetables are cooking, prepare the vinaigrette. Combine 1/4 cup olive oil, the vinegar, sumac, orange zest and juice, a pinch of salt and some freshly ground pepper in the bottom of a large salad bowl and whisk together. Set aside.

5 When the vegetables are ready, remove from the oven and add to the salad bowl. Toss well to coat with the vinaigrette.

Roasted Carrots, Parsnips, Zucchini and Onion Salad

This is a salad that can be eaten hot, cold or at room temperature. It's also great the next day. The salad tends to be a little different each time you make it — at least it is each time I make it. I use the ingredients I have in my fridge at the time, so there may be more zucchini in it or carrots or parsnips depending on the season and what I found at the market.

I'd love to say that all these vegetables come out of my garden, but my green thumb only seems to stretch as far as herbs and flowers, a few tomatoes and a little chard. My zucchini plants failed completely this year, and I was really looking forward to the patty pan squash I planted. Oh well, maybe next year.

Serves 8 to 10 people

For the vegetables:

3-4 patty pan squash — ends trimmed and then cut into wedges — try to use different varieties

2-3 green zucchini — ends trimmed, split lengthways and then sliced

4-5 carrots — peeled and sliced

4 small to medium parsnips — peeled, quartered and sliced

1 large red onion — peeled, halved and cut into thin slices

Juice of 2 lemons

5-6 sprigs of thyme

Olive oil

Sea salt and black pepper

For the herb pesto:

4 tablespoons fruity olive oil

Juice and zest of 2 lemons

1 large handful parsley — chopped

1 large handful cilantro — roughly chopped

1 large handful basil leaves

2 tablespoons chives — chopped

1 clove garlic

1 Preheat the oven to 375 degrees.

2 Place all the vegetables in a roasting pan and drizzle with olive oil. Squeeze the lemons over the vegetables and add the thyme, a dash or two of salt and 4-5 grinds of pepper. Roast the vegetables in the oven for 25-30 minutes. The carrots and zucchini can have a little crunch, but the parsnips do need to be cooked through, so check those in particular.

3 While the vegetables are roasting, prepare the herb pesto. Place all the pesto ingredients into a blender or food processor (liquids first — it makes it easier to process the pesto) and run it until you have a relatively smooth pesto. Check the seasoning. Depending on the size of the lemons you use, you may need a dash more. It should be bright green and very fresh tasting. Pour the pesto into a salad bowl and add the roasted vegetables to the bowl as soon as they are cooked. Toss while they are still warm.

Carrot, Radish and Orange Salad

Suddenly, there are versions of this salad everywhere. This is my take on this crunchy, juicy and peppery salad. You can use blood oranges when they are in season and different varieties of radishes for a little variation.

Serves 8 people

4 oranges — peeled and
    thinly sliced into disks

4 carrots — peeled and
    very thinly sliced

8-10 radishes — washed
    and thinly sliced

1/4 cup olive oil

Juice of 1/2 lemon

1 teaspoon orange flower
    water

1 pinch cumin

1 pinch cinnamon

Coarse sea salt

Black pepper

1/2 bunch chives —
    finely chopped

1 Place the sliced oranges, carrots and radishes on a platter and arrange them in an appealing pattern.

2 In a separate bowl, mix together all the remaining ingredients except for the chives. Whisk the mixture together well to form an emulsion.

3 Pour the vinaigrette over the oranges and then sprinkle with the chives a good 10 minutes before you serve the salad.

ENDIVE & FENNEL

Endive and
Microgreen Salad

—

Summer Salad

—

Fennel, Endive and
Walnut Salad

—

Fennel, Endive and
Smoked Salmon
Salad

—

Santa Barbara
Red Rock Crab with
a Shaved Fennel
Salad and Avocado
Vinaigrette

—

Endive and Fig Salad

—

Fennel, Arugula and
Mint Salad with
Shaved Pecorino

Endive and Microgreen Salad

I took my daughter to Thomas Keller's Bouchon Bistro in Los Angeles for her sixteenth birthday. She was thrilled; so was I. The bistro resembles a large Parisian brasserie, shades of Lipp or La Coupole, complete with high vaulted ceilings, tiled floors and waiters gliding around with starched calf-length white aprons. The menu is classic bistro fare. The chef had a salad on the menu that was his play on the classic endive-walnut-blue cheese combination, using big chunks of blue cheese, whole toasted walnuts and both red and white Belgian endives that were stacked in an appealing manner. This dish is inspired by that visit.

Serves 8 people

5 tablespoons olive oil

1 tablespoon sherry vinegar

Sea salt and pepper to taste

Juice and zest of 1 lemon

6 endives — cored and leaves left whole

1 apple — a sweet crunchy one — peeled, cored and thinly sliced

3–4 oz microgreens

4 oz pistachios or almonds or a mixture of both — roughly chopped

6 oz feta cheese (optional)

1 Combine the olive oil, vinegar, lemon zest and juice, a pinch of salt and some pepper in a large bowl and whisk together vigorously. Place the endive leaves and apples in the bowl and toss very gently. The endive leaves can be a little delicate.

2 Divide the endives and apples between eight plates and stack them in a cross-hatch pattern. Sprinkle each plate with some of the microgreens and the nuts. Grind some black pepper and crumble the cheese on top.

Summer Salad

My good friend Sherry arrived at my house one day with three ears of beautiful, just-picked corn. It really did not need cooking at all as the kernels were so sweet and juicy. We chopped up a bunch of other vegetables so that they were all kernel-size and made a quick summer salad. You can make the same salad with grilled corn, which I also like, bringing some of the char-grilled flavors to the mix.

Serves 8 people

1 tablespoon Dijon mustard

4 tablespoons olive oil

1 tablespoon white wine vinegar

Sea salt and black pepper

3 ears fresh corn — try to find the multi-colored type if you can

4 small Belgian endives — leaves removed and left whole

1 small-medium daikon radish — diced

1 green apple — peeled, cored and diced

½ English cucumber — peeled and diced

2 tablespoons chives — finely diced

1 tablespoon chopped dill — finely diced

1 Combine the mustard, olive oil, vinegar, a good pinch of salt and some pepper in the bottom of a large bowl.

2 Steam the corn for 4–5 minutes. Remove from the stove and shuck the corn. Place the kernels into the bowl with the vinaigrette.

3 Add all the remaining ingredients and toss together well, taking care with the endive leaves as they can be a little delicate.

Fennel, Endive and Walnut Salad

Endive and blue cheese are a natural food pairing, akin to port and Stilton or Sauternes and Roquefort. I think that fennel and blue cheese fall into that same category. Here, the vegetables are combined with herbs and nuts for a rustic, fresh, crisp salad.

Serves 8 people

1 rounded tablespoon Dijon mustard

¼ cup olive oil

2 tablespoons vinegar — such as apple bouquet vinegar or Jerez vinegar

Sea salt and black pepper

1 large fennel bulb — cut in half and thinly sliced

3 endives — cut in half and thinly sliced

3 apples — choose a crunchy variety that is a little sweet such as Gala — cut into thin slices

8 oz mache greens

4 oz nuts — walnuts, cashews or pistachios or a mix — roughly chopped

4 oz golden raisins

6 oz blue cheese — such as Fourme d'Ambert or other variety of mild blue cheese

2 tablespoons parsley — finely chopped

1 tablespoon chives — finely chopped

2 tablespoons small mint leaves — left whole (if the leaves are large, cut them in half)

1 Place the mustard in a large salad bowl. Drizzle in the olive oil and whisk until you have a thick vinaigrette with the consistency of mayonnaise. Add the vinegar in the same manner. Taste and season with a little salt and pepper.

2 Place salad servers over the vinaigrette and then place all the salad ingredients on top of the salad servers, ensuring that the ingredients do not fall into the vinaigrette. When you are ready to serve the salad, toss it gently so that everything is well combined.

Fennel, Endive and Smoked Salmon Salad

I really like good smoked salmon. It's one of those foods that I rarely get tired of, be it on toast with a squeeze of lemon, with a poached egg, with scrambled eggs, in a soufflé, in a sandwich, on a flatbread or on a pizza. I'm beginning to sound like Sam I Am and his green eggs and ham, but there are really very few things that I would not eat smoked salmon with. Adding salmon to salads lends a certain elegance and richness to the dish. I love it every time.

Serves 8 people

1/4 cup pistachios —
     roughly chopped

1/4 cup olive oil

1 tablespoon red wine
     vinegar

Pinch of sea salt and black
     pepper

4 endives — halved and
     thinly sliced crosswise

1 large fennel bulb — fronds
     trimmed, quartered and
     thinly sliced crosswise

2 large handfuls mesclun
     salad mix

1 tablespoon olives—
     finely sliced

8 oz smoked salmon —
     cut into thin strips

2 tablespoons dill —
     finely chopped

1/4 cup parsley —
     finely chopped

1 bunch chives —
     finely chopped

1 Place a heavy-bottomed pan over medium heat. When the pan is hot, add the pistachios and dry roast them for 2–3 minutes. Remove the pan from the heat and add the olive oil and vinegar. Whisk together well. Pour the vinaigrette with the nuts into the bottom of a large salad bowl. Add a pinch of salt and some black pepper. Place serving utensils over the vinaigrette.

2 Place the remaining ingredients on top of the utensils. When you are ready to serve the salad, toss it gently so that everything is well combined.

NOTE: If you don't have smoked salmon, you can substitute cooked salmon filet.

Santa Barbara Red Rock Crab with a Shaved Fennel Salad and Avocado Vinaigrette

I once taught a class with a dynamic young woman who used to wholesale fish. She would work directly with the local fishermen so her product literally came straight off the boat. She called me one day and said she had some great local crab. This is the salad we made together. The avocado vinaigrette is buttery and works wonders with the crab and fennel.

Serves 8 people

For the crab:

16 crab claws

1 tablespoon chopped chives

1 lemon — cut into 8 wedges

For the vinaigrette:

¼ cup olive oil

1 tablespoon apple cider vinegar or Champagne vinegar

1 avocado — peeled and the meat scooped out

1 tablespoon lemon juice

Pinch of sea salt and black pepper

1 tablespoon freshly chopped parsley

For the fennel salad:

2 whole fennel bulbs — cut in half lengthwise and very thinly sliced

1 lemon — zested and then quartered

1 tablespoon fresh dill — finely chopped

1 small green apple — cored and very thinly sliced

1 tablespoon chives — finely chopped

Flake salt

1 Steam the crab claws for 15–18 minutes.

2 Place some newspaper on a counter or table. Remove the crab claws from the steamer and place on the newspaper. Lay each claw flat on the paper. Hold the claw with a dishcloth and use a mallet to firmly crack open the shell. Extricate the crab meat.

3 For the vinaigrette, pour the olive oil into a small bowl and whisk in the vinegar. Add the avocado meat and mash with a fork. Add the lemon juice, parsley, salt and 2–3 grinds of pepper and whisk with the fork so that all the ingredients form a homogeneous vinaigrette.

4 Place the fennel, lemon zest, dill, apples and chives into a medium-sized bowl and toss with the vinaigrette.

5 To serve, place a spoonful of the fennel salad in the center of each plate, and then place the crab meat on top. Add a little salt and pepper, a sprinkling of freshly chopped chives, a squeeze of fresh lemon juice and serve immediately.

Endive and Fig Salad

I have written about my neighbor's fig tree before. It literally drips with figs. Every time I walk past the tree, I am so, so tempted to pluck one from the overhanging branches, but have resisted temptation. Instead, I rely on the beautiful figs from the farmers' market. I love sweet figs and slightly bitter endives together; they make a great salad. You can make this salad with or without cheese. I found that goat cheese, feta or Queso de Valdeón work well.

Serves 8 to 10 people

For the endives:

½ bunch cilantro leaves

3 tablespoons olive oil

1 tablespoon lemon juice

Pinch of coarse sea salt

6 large Belgian endives — cut in half and leaves removed from the core but left whole

For the fig salad:

3 tablespoons olive oil

1 tablespoon apple cider vinegar

2 pints assorted figs — each fig cut into eighths

4 Asian pears — peeled and thinly sliced

3 green onions — very thinly sliced

4 oz baby arugula

4 oz Queso de Valdeón — crumbled (optional)

1   Combine the cilantro, olive oil, lemon juice and salt in the bottom of a large bowl and whisk together. Place salad servers over the vinaigrette and add the endive leaves.

2   When ready to assemble the salad, remove the salad utensils and let the endive leaves fall into the vinaigrette, then very gently toss the leaves. You want them to remain whole and not bruise.

3   Arrange 10–12 of the endive leaves on a salad plate in the shape of a flower so that the root end of each leaf is in the center of the plate. Repeat with each of the eight plates.

4   For the fig salad, pour the olive oil and apple cider vinegar into a large bowl and whisk together. Place serving utensils over the vinaigrette. Place all the remaining ingredients on top of the utensils, except for the cheese.

5   After you have prepared the plates with the endive flowers and are ready to serve the salad, carefully toss the fig salad. Divide it equally into eight portions. Mound it in the center of each of the endive flowers. Crumble the cheese on top of each salad.

Fennel, Arugula and Mint Salad with Shaved Pecorino

You can often find a simple arugula salad with shaved Pecorino in Italian restaurants. This salad takes that concept a little further. I like the marriage of the peppercorns and the cheese with the spicy-pepperiness of the radishes and the arugula. Try different cheeses in the salad, too — perhaps some Manchego or Parmesan, and use a cheese slicer to get thin curled pieces of cheese. They look gorgeous on the salad.

Serves 8 people

1/4 cup olive oil

1 tablespoon balsamic vinegar

Sea salt and cracked black peppercorns

3 large fennel bulbs — halved lengthwise and finely diced

3-4 radishes — thinly sliced

3-4 shallots — peeled and very finely diced

6 oz arugula

1 bunch chives — finely chopped

1 bunch mint leaves — try to use small leaves, left whole

4 oz Pecorino cheese — shaved

1 Pour the olive oil and vinegar into the bottom of a large salad bowl. Whisk together until you have an emulsion. Add a good pinch of sea salt and some freshly ground pepper and whisk again. Place salad servers on top of the vinaigrette.

2 Place all of the remaining ingredients (except for the cheese) on top of the salad servers. When you are ready to serve, use the utensils to toss the salad. Divide the salad between the dinner plates and top each with the shaved cheese. This is delicious served with some warm olive bread or a baguette.

FIGS

Roasted Figs Stuffed
with Goat Cheese and
a Herb Salad

—

Fig Tapenade Crostini
with a Watercress
Salad

—

Fig, Grape and
Ricotta Salad

—

Fig and Prosciutto
Salad

—

Fig and Tomato
Salad with Purple
Basil

Roasted Figs Stuffed with Goat Cheese and a Herb Salad

A ripe fig is like a good book hiding behind a plain cover, albeit one with beautiful coloring. Open it up and delve inside and you find hidden treasures — nature's poetry enveloped in a small, plum-sized case. Ripe figs are sweet, honey scented, floral and tender, filled with tiny seeds that feel a little granular beneath your teeth. They are the perfect foil for savory partners such as prosciutto, cheese and nuts. In this salad, the goat cheese added to the warmed figs melts into the center and creates little mouthfuls of fig heaven.

Serves 8 people

For the figs:

24 figs

2 tablespoons olive oil

8 oz goat cheese

For the vinaigrette:

2 tablespoons olive oil

1 tablespoon lemon juice

1/2 tablespoon fig balsamic vinegar

1/2 tablespoon pear Champagne vinegar or red wine vinegar

For the salad:

1/2 bunch chives — finely chopped

8 oz fresh salad greens

1/2 bunch purple basil leaves

2 tablespoons cilantro leaves

2 tablespoons dill — finely chopped

Sea salt and black pepper

1 Preheat the oven to 350 degrees.

2 Carefully make a cross-cut into the top of each fig. Do not cut all the way through. Place the figs into a baking pan, and drizzle a little olive oil into each one. Sprinkle with a little salt and pepper.

3 Place in the oven and roast for 10 minutes, or just until the fig starts to unfold like a flower.

4 While the figs are roasting, prepare the vinaigrette and herb salad.

5 Pour the olive oil and lemon juice into a large salad bowl. Whisk in the vinegar, a pinch of salt and some black pepper to create an emulsified vinaigrette. Place salad servers over the vinaigrette.

6 Place all the salad greens and herbs in the bowl, on top of the serving utensils.

7 After the figs have roasted for 10 minutes, remove them from the oven and insert some goat cheese into the top of each one. Return the figs to the oven and cook for another 5 minutes.

8 To serve, toss the salad and divide it equally between the salad plates. Place 3 figs on top of each salad. Serve while the figs are still warm.

Fig Tapenade Crostini with a Watercress Salad

This is what you make when you either have too many figs or too many ripe figs. Olives and figs are oddly wonderful together — it's that whole salty-sweet thing that works so well. You can also serve the crostini as an appetizer.

Serves 8 people

For the crostini:

1 cup black olives — pitted

1 teaspoon capers

1 clove garlic — chopped

Juice and zest of 1 lemon

8-10 fresh figs

Olive oil

Baguette or ciabatta — cut into thin slices and toasted

1/2 bunch chives — finely chopped

For the salad:

3 tablespoons olive oil

Juice of 1 lemon

Sea salt and black pepper

4–6 oz watercress (use some watercress microgreens too, if you can find them)

24 small green figs — halved

1 Place the olives, capers, garlic, lemon juice and zest and 8-10 figs in a food processor and pulse until you have a coarse tapenade.

2 Drizzle a little olive oil onto each slice of toast and spoon some of the tapenade onto the toasts. Sprinkle the tops of each crostini with some of the chopped chives.

3 For the watercress salad, whisk the olive oil and lemon juice together in a small bowl. Season with a little salt and pepper.

4 Divide the watercress greens between eight plates and arrange the rest of the figs on top of the greens. Drizzle with the vinaigrette. Place 2 or 3 crostini onto each plate and serve.

Fig, Grape and Ricotta Salad

I had planned to make a fig and buffalo mozzarella salad for dinner. You know, the one where you slowly tear pieces of fresh mozzarella apart, pop it on a plate, add some figs and drizzle with a little olive oil. That was the plan, until my lovely friend Nancy arrived with some truly incredible seedless grapes from her garden. She and her husband have magic soil and produce sumptuous veggies and fruit. The grapes were bursting with flavor and were sweet and juicy. I decided I had to add them to the salad too, along with these crunchy, slightly salty, blistered almonds I picked up at the farmers' market. If you can get your hands on the blistered almonds from Fat Uncle Farms — do. They are incredible.

I had intended to pick up the mozzarella but got completely sidetracked by the fresh ricotta I spied in the cheese shop. Um... fresh ricotta with figs, the grapes, the almonds and some arugula for a little zing in the salad. Ricotta in hand, I rushed home and made this salad. I've made it with crumbled feta cheese, which works well, too. Both versions are yummy.

Serves 8 people

4 oz arugula

32 figs — quartered

1 bunch grapes — halved

3 oz salted almonds

½ lb fresh ricotta

Zest and juice of 2 lemons

1 tablespoon honey

5 tablespoons olive oil

Sea salt and black pepper

1 Divide the arugula between eight dinner plates. Scatter the figs, grapes and almonds over the arugula. Dot the top of each salad with some of the fresh ricotta.

2 Combine the lemon zest and juice, honey, olive oil, a pinch of salt and 4–5 grinds of fresh black pepper in a small bowl and whisk together vigorously. You want the honey to be completely incorporated into the other ingredients, otherwise it just tends to sit at the bottom of the bowl. When you are ready to serve, pour a little of the vinaigrette over each plate.

Fig and Prosciutto Salad

This is one of the salads I usually make as soon as I get back to my father's house in France. One of the first things I do there is to go to the market. By market, I mean one that takes place outdoors and not a shop. This market takes place twice a week, on Tuesday and Saturday mornings in a bucolic, tree-lined square. It is one of my all-time favorite places to be. I love meandering through the colorful aisles, feasting on all the delicacies. I'll pick up olives, tapenade, some bread, such as *fougasse* and *pain aux noix*; a sampling of fresh goat cheese, made in the previous 48 hours, from what has to be the best cheese shop on wheels in Provence; and some prosciutto. This is prosciutto that melts in your mouth. It is very hard not to polish off the entire carefully-wrapped package before I get home — particularly, as I also have that just-baked, slightly warm piece of bread in my basket. Add to this some vegetables and fruit, and we're ready for lunch. I'll make a small green salad to go with this, eat some of the goat cheese and munch on the bread. This is my idea of the perfect day.

Serves 8 people

16 ripe figs — some left whole, some halved, some quartered

16 slices prosciutto

4 oz olives — pitted, left whole

1 small bunch chives — finely chopped

4 oz Manchego — shaved into thin slices

Large handful basil leaves

Sea salt and black pepper

3 tablespoons olive oil

1 tablespoon red wine vinegar

1 Arrange the prosciutto on a large serving platter. Dot the surface of the prosciutto with the figs and olives. Sprinkle the chives over the top.

2 Add the Manchego shavings, the basil leaves, a pinch of salt and some pepper.

3 Combine the olive oil and vinegar in a small bowl and whisk together well. Drizzle the vinaigrette over the salad and serve.

Fig and Tomato Salad with Purple Basil

This salad came about one day when, for no particular reason, I sliced figs horizontally instead of in the more traditional quarters. All these exquisite ruby-colored fig disks were strewn on my cutting board. I sliced some tomatoes in the same manner and arranged them on a plate, drizzled some olive oil over the top, added a couple of purple basil leaves from the garden and sat down to lunch. This salad, along with the peach and tomato salad, are now two of my summer favorites.

Serves 8 people

1 lb assorted tomatoes

1 basket figs — assorted if possible (smile sweetly at the farmer and he might create a mixed basket for you)

1 bunch purple basil leaves

A good fruity olive oil

Coarse sea salt

Black pepper

1 Carefully wash all the tomatoes and figs. The larger tomatoes should be handled with care as they can bruise easily.

2 Using a serrated knife or a very sharp knife, slice the tomatoes horizontally. Arrange them on a dinner plate, mixing the varieties and colors so that they cover the entire surface.

3 Prepare the figs. Cut each fig into thin slices, the same way you sliced the tomatoes. This creates a great looking pattern.

4 Carefully insert the assorted fig slices between the tomato slices.

5 Insert the whole basil leaves between the fruit and then drizzle a little olive oil over the entire salad. Sprinkle some coarse sea salt and grind some black pepper over the entire dish.

GRAINS & RICE

Couscous Salad

—

Israeli Couscous
with Pine Nuts and
Golden Shallots

—

Watercress Tabouleh

Forbidden Rice with
Grilled Brussels
Sprouts

—

Red Quinoa with
Blood Oranges,
Pistachios, Herbs and
Thyme-Encrusted
Roasted Duck Legs

—

Multi-Colored
Quinoa Salad with
Roasted Portobello
Mushrooms

—

Quinoa and Zucchini
Salad

Couscous Salad

Thought to have originated in North Africa, couscous — which is made from rolling semolina (the heart of durum wheat) into a fine grain — is one of the traditional dishes of Morocco, Tunisia and Algeria. It's usually cooked with vegetables and some meat, herbs and a variety of spices. As couscous has become more widely available and easier to prepare, its popularity has spread worldwide.

I like to use couscous in salads and incorporate the herbs, fruits and vegetables I have on hand. If apricots are not in season, you can use dried apricots or peaches instead. You can also use different herbs such as parsley or cilantro. Couscous is a wonderful picnic food.

Serves 8 people

3 tablespoons olive oil

2 cups couscous (uncooked)

1 red onion — peeled and thinly sliced

1/3 cup dried cranberries or cherries

Zest of 1 lemon

1 large bunch chives — finely chopped

1/4 cup pistachios — chopped

1 tablespoon red wine vinegar

Coarse sea salt

6 apricots — each cut into 8 pieces

1 Bring 2 cups salted water and 1 tablespoon olive oil to a boil in a large saucepan. Add the couscous, cover, remove from the heat and let sit for 10 minutes. Remove the lid and fluff the couscous with a fork.

2 While the couscous is cooking, pour a little olive oil into a medium-sized skillet placed over medium heat. Add the red onion and dried cranberries and sauté until soft and translucent — about 4 minutes. Stir in the chives, pistachios and lemon zest, and cook for 1 minute more. Remove from the heat.

3 Combine the olive oil and vinegar and a pinch of salt in the bottom of a medium-sized salad bowl. Add the red onion mixture to the vinaigrette and toss to combine. Add the cooked couscous and the chopped apricots. Carefully toss the salad so that the apricots do not get squished.

Israeli Couscous with Pine Nuts and Golden Shallots

Israeli couscous is really a misnomer as this starch is neither Israeli in origin nor traditional couscous. It's a form of pasta and is known as *ptitim* in Israel where it is primarily a children's food. The Turks, Palestinians, Sardinians and Lebanese all have versions of this dish, some made from pearled barley and some, like Israeli couscous, made from a combination of wheat, eggs and water. It became popular in Israel during the 1950s and has become a staple since then. You can usually find it in most gourmet grocery shops.

Israeli couscous has a chewy, slightly nutty flavor. In addition to making salads with it, you can serve it with all sorts of sauces — pesto being one of my favorites — or perhaps a chunky tomato-olive sauce. You can also add all sorts of herbs to the couscous and drizzle it with a fruity olive oil. This salad can be served alongside some grilled vegetables or with grilled fish or any roasts, particularly pork, chicken and duck.

Serves 8 people

1 tablespoon olive oil

4–5 shallots — peeled and sliced

8 oz dried Israeli couscous

1 3/4 cups boiling water

14-16 dates — halved and sliced

3 tablespoons chives — finely chopped

4–5 tablespoons parsley — finely chopped

2 oz pine nuts — lightly toasted

Olive oil

Sea salt and black pepper

1   Pour the olive oil into a large saucepan placed over medium heat. Add the chopped shallots and cook 4–5 minutes, stirring occasionally, until lightly golden.

2   Add the couscous to the shallots and cook, stirring frequently, for 4–5 minutes. The couscous should be lightly browned.

3   Add the boiling water to the couscous, and reduce heat to medium-low and cover. Simmer for 12 minutes or until the liquid is absorbed. Place the cooked couscous and shallots in a bowl.

4   When ready to serve, add the dates, chives, parsley and toasted pine nuts to the couscous. Drizzle a little olive oil over the couscous, add some salt and pepper and stir to combine.

Watercress Tabouleh

Purists would give me a hard time calling this dish tabouleh, which is traditionally made with bulgur, has tomatoes and cucumber in it and is filled with masses of herbs. My interpretation is made with couscous grains instead of bulgur, and with lots of watercress plus a few spices and some dates. Not traditional, but yummy nonetheless.

The original versions stem from Lebanon and Syria, where couscous is usually part of the *mezze* (appetizer) table. It's really a herb salad with a little bit of bulgur added. This version is half and half. If you prefer the bright green herb salad, use half the quantity of couscous (or bulgur) and increase the amount of herbs.

Serves 8 people

1 cup water

1 cup couscous (you can also make this with fine bulgur, although the preparation of the bulgur is slightly different)

1 tablespoon butter

Large pinch of sea salt

1 large red onion — peeled and finely chopped

1 teaspoon cumin

1/2 teaspoon ground cardamom

3 bunches watercress leaves — finely sliced

1 large bunch fresh mint leaves — finely sliced

1 large bunch chives — finely chopped

1/2 bunch parsley — finely chopped

1 medium-sized yellow tomato — finely diced

Juice and zest of 2 lemons

1/3 cup olive oil

Sea salt and black pepper

1 In a large saucepan, bring the water to a boil. Add the couscous, salt and butter; cover and remove from the heat. Leave covered for 10 minutes. Remove the lid and fluff the couscous with a fork. Transfer the cooked couscous to a bowl.

2 While the couscous is cooking, pour a little olive oil into a medium-sized skillet placed over medium heat. Add the finely diced red onion, the cumin and cardamom and cook, stirring frequently, until the onions are completely soft, about 8-10 minutes. Add the onions to the cooked couscous.

3 When the couscous and onion mixture has cooled to room temperature, stir in the herbs. When you are ready to serve the couscous, sprinkle it with the lemon juice, add the olive oil, some salt and pepper, and toss.

Forbidden Rice with Grilled Brussels Sprouts

Ah, forbidden rice. Ancient Chinese legend has it that if you were caught eating black rice you would face severe consequences, as this was the food of the Emperor's court. Thankfully, we can now all partake of this delicious nutty rice without fear of losing our heads. Black rice turns an incredible deep, deep purple color when cooked. It's packed with antioxidants and anthocyanins, so it's good for you, but most of all, it's really rather delicious.

About Brussels sprouts: When I lived in London, there was a Scottish woman who lived in the ground-floor flat beneath ours. She "killed" vegetables on an almost daily basis, literally boiling them to death for hours on end, voiding them of any nutritional value at all. The worst days were when she cooked cabbage or Brussels sprouts. The extraordinary smell of rotting socks would hit you like a mallet as soon as you walked in the door; the offending aromas would penetrate every floor of the house. I did not eat Brussels sprouts for a very long time.

I promise that these are a far cry from any childhood horror. For those of you who still cannot eat (or bear the thought of) Brussels sprouts, you can make this salad with grilled zucchini or grilled corn. I won't hold it against you.

Serves 8 people

1 lb black rice (forbidden rice) — rinsed in cold water

3 cups water

1 1/2 lbs Brussels sprouts

Zest and juice of 2 lemons

3 tablespoons olive oil

Sea salt and black pepper

1 bunch chives — thinly sliced

1 bunch spring onions — ends trimmed and then stalks thinly sliced

1 Place the rice and water into a large saucepan placed over high heat. Add a pinch of salt and bring to a boil. As soon as the water boils, cover and reduce to a simmer. Cook for approximately 25 minutes or until the rice is tender and the water has been absorbed.

2 While the rice is cooking, prepare the Brussels sprouts. Bring a large saucepan of water to a boil. Pop the sprouts in the water and cook for 2 minutes. Drain the sprouts. When cool enough to handle, halve them. Place the cut sprouts into a bowl and drizzle with a little olive oil, a pinch of salt and some pepper. Toss to coat.

3 Heat a cast-iron grill pan. Add the Brussels sprouts and cook for 2–3 minutes on each side. They will still be a little crunchy. Once cooked, place the Brussels sprouts into a medium-sized salad bowl.

4 Add the cooked rice to the salad bowl with the Brussels sprouts. Pour the lemon juice and olive oil over the rice and sprouts mixture. Scatter the chives, spring onions and lemon zest on top, grind some black pepper over the salad and toss all the ingredients together well.

Red Quinoa with Blood Oranges, Pistachios, Herbs and Thyme-Encrusted Roasted Duck Legs

The first time I ate quinoa, I was intrigued by its grain-like texture and fine, slightly earthy taste. I wanted to find out more about this seed. It has been cultivated for more than 3,000 years in the Andes and was prized by the Inca. It grows in very inhospitable places and has to be harvested and threshed by hand. I appreciate every mouthful all the more, knowing the extraordinary efforts made by quinoa farmers to bring their crop to market.

It is a diverse seed that works well in salads; you can substitute it for couscous, for example, or in a tabouleh for a more rustic dish. The earthiness pairs well with oranges and other fruit and with the richness of the duck. This dish is a favorite at home.

Serves 8 to 10 people

8 duck legs — trimmed of as much fat as possible

1 bunch fresh thyme

Sea salt and black pepper

2 cups red quinoa

2 cups water

5-6 shallots — peeled and thinly sliced

Zest of 4 blood oranges — the oranges also need to be peeled and the fruit chopped into very small pieces

1 tablespoon red wine vinegar or balsamic vinegar

1/2 cup pistachios

1 bunch chives — finely chopped

1/4 cup parsley — finely chopped

2 blood oranges — quartered

1 Preheat the oven to 350 degrees.

2 Place the duck legs on a sheet pan and carefully score the skin side of each leg, cutting slightly into the meat. Insert a sprig of thyme into each incision. Sprinkle coarse sea salt and some black pepper over each leg. Place the pan in the center of the oven. Roast for 1 hour.

3 While the duck is cooking, prepare the quinoa. Place the quinoa in a saucepan with 2 cups of water and bring to a boil. Reduce to a simmer, cover and cook until the quinoa has absorbed all the water. You can also cook the quinoa in a rice cooker, using the same proportions.

4 While the quinoa is cooking, sauté the shallots with a little olive oil in a shallow, heavy-bottomed pan placed over medium heat. Cook until soft and translucent. Stir the orange zest into the shallots. Add a pinch of salt, some pepper and the vinegar. Set aside.

5 As soon as the quinoa is cooked, place it into a warmed serving dish and combine it with the cooked shallots, the orange pieces, pistachios and the chopped herbs. Toss to combine so that all the ingredients are well distributed throughout the quinoa.

6 To serve, spoon some of the quinoa onto the center of each dinner plate and top with a roasted duck leg. Squeeze the quartered blood oranges over each duck leg and serve at once.

Multi-Colored Quinoa Salad with Roasted Portobello Mushrooms

This salad combines the earthiness of mushrooms and quinoa. I like to make it when I come across some freshly picked mushrooms at the market, especially chanterelles or beautiful shiitake.

Serves 8 people

For the quinoa:

1 cup quinoa — carefully rinsed

2 cups water

Olive oil

1 medium-sized yellow onion — finely chopped

1 lb wild greens such as baby bok choy, dandelion greens, kale, or rapini — finely chopped

Sea salt and black pepper

1/3 cup blistered almonds — chopped

2 tablespoons chives — finely chopped

2 tablespoons parsley — finely chopped

2 tablespoons cilantro — finely chopped

For the mushrooms:

1/4 cup olive oil

1 tablespoon balsamic vinegar

1 teaspoon smoked salt such as Salish

1 tablespoon chives — finely chopped

8 large portobello mushrooms — stems removed, caps left intact

2 tablespoons butter

1/2 lb shiitake, chanterelles or other wild mushrooms — stems removed and thinly sliced

1/4 lb Stilton or other blue cheese such as Roquefort or Gorgonzola

1 Place the quinoa in a saucepan with the water and bring to a boil. Reduce to a simmer, cover and cook until the quinoa has absorbed all the water. You can also cook the quinoa in a rice cooker, using the same proportions.

2 Pour a little olive oil into a large skillet placed over medium heat. Add the onion and cook until soft and translucent. Add the greens and cook for 5–7 minutes. They should still be bright green. Add a little pinch of salt and some pepper and stir.

3 Once the greens are cooked, add the cooked quinoa, chopped almonds and all of the herbs. Combine well.

4 Preheat the oven to 400 degrees.

5 Combine the olive oil, vinegar, a good pinch of the smoked salt and chives in a bowl. Whisk together well. Add the portobello mushrooms to the bowl and carefully toss the mushrooms, taking care not to break them. Do this at least 30 minutes prior to baking them.

6 Place the mushrooms cap side down on a baking sheet and bake in the oven for 20 minutes.

7 While the portobello mushrooms are cooking, add the butter to a skillet placed over medium heat. Once the butter has melted, add the remaining wild mushrooms and sauté until just browned.

8 Remove the portobello mushrooms from the oven and spoon some of the sautéed mushrooms into the center of each portobello mushroom. Place some of the Stilton (or other blue cheese) on top, and return to the oven for 5–7 minutes more to allow the cheese to melt.

9 To serve, spoon some of the quinoa salad into the center of each dinner plate and place one of the large filled portobello mushrooms on top. Serve while hot.

Quinoa and Zucchini Salad

I first made this salad for a picnic I prepared for Zaca Mesa Winery in the Santa Ynez Valley. We traveled down a long dusty road through the vines to get to the idyllic picnic spot that's situated beneath large oak trees. As we unfolded tablecloths and unpacked the food, a gentle breeze came drifting through the vines. It was a prelude to a beautiful afternoon where guests sampled wines and ate a languorous meal. All that was needed were hammocks in which to take a siesta.

Serves 8 people

2 cups red quinoa — rinsed
    and drained

2 cups water

2 yellow onions — peeled
    and finely diced

4–5 zucchini — ends
    trimmed away and diced

1 bunch green onions —
    ends trimmed and then
    stalks finely sliced

Sea salt and pepper

1 tablespoon vegetable herb
    mix (see suppliers) or
    Herbes de Provence

Juice and zest of 1 lemon

1 tablespoon Jerez vinegar
    or red wine vinegar

4 tablespoons olive oil

2 handfuls of cilantro leaves
    — left whole

3 tablespoons pistachios

1 bunch chives —
    finely chopped

Juice of 2 lemons

1 Preheat the oven to 350 degrees.

2 Place the quinoa and water in a saucepan and bring to a boil. Reduce to a simmer, cover and cook until the quinoa has absorbed all the water. You can also cook the quinoa in a rice cooker, using the same proportions.

3 Place the onions, zucchini and green onions into a baking dish. Drizzle with a little olive oil, 1 tablespoon of vegetable herb mix or Herbes de Provence, some salt and pepper, and roast in the oven for 45 minutes.

4 In a medium-sized salad bowl, whisk the lemon juice, lemon zest, vinegar and olive oil together until well combined. Once the quinoa is cooked, add it and the roasted vegetables, chives, cilantro and pistachios to the salad bowl and toss all together. Serve while still warm.

FAVA BEANS, HARICOTS VERTS & PEAS

Haricots Verts Salad

~

PB Salad

~

Fava Bean, Spring Pea and Almond Salad

~

Watercress and Spring Pea Salad

~

Cherry, Pea and Fava Bean Salad

Haricots Verts Salad

This is another one of those classic French salads. Every time my grandmother or my mother made a roasted leg of lamb, she would serve this alongside. I love the slight bite of the shallots and mustard vinaigrette with the dainty haricots verts.

Serves 8 people

2 lbs haricots verts —
    ends trimmed

2 shallots — peeled and
    finely chopped

Sea salt and black pepper

1 tablespoon Dijon mustard

4 tablespoons olive oil

1 tablespoon white wine
    vinegar or tarragon
    vinegar

I bunch chives —
    finely chopped

1 Place the haricots verts in a steamer and cook for 5-7 minutes. The haricots verts should still be bright green and al dente. As soon as they are cooked, remove them from the steamer and rinse under cold water. Drain.

2 Place the shallots in a small bowl with a good pinch of salt and some pepper. Stir the shallots and the salt and leave for 5 minutes before making the vinaigrette. (This helps soften the flavor of the shallots.)

3 Combine the mustard, olive oil and vinegar in a salad bowl and whisk together to create an emulsion. Add the shallots, the cooked haricots verts and the chives, and toss well to combine.

PB Salad

Walking through the Santa Barbara Farmers Market on an early Saturday morning, I came across a bunch of edible nasturtiums. They ranged in color from sunflower yellow to pumpkin orange and proved to be irresistible. Lying in the basket next to them were some pea tendrils. If you have never had them, please try to find some. They taste absolutely fresh and delicious when lightly sautéed in a little olive oil with a squeeze of lemon juice. They are also a versatile addition to many salads.

I had a couple of bunches of golden beets in my basket and imagined all these colorful ingredients coming together in a salad bowl. When I spied the fava beans, my salad was complete — in my mind that is.

My lovely Mum was coming over for lunch later that day, and this is the salad I made for her. The PB stands for peas and beets.

Serves 8 people

Olive oil

6 medium-sized golden beets — peeled and thinly sliced on a mandolin

1 teaspoon white wine vinegar or pear Champagne vinegar

1 large red onion — peeled, quartered and thinly sliced

1 lb snap peas — thinly sliced on a bias

1 lb fava beans — shelled (you will need to remove the bean from the pod and then the outer shell of the fava bean — it's easier if you blanch them first for 2 minutes)

1 large bunch pea tendrils — roughly chopped

3 tablespoons orange juice (blood orange if possible)

3 tablespoons olive oil

1 tablespoon fig balsamic vinegar

Sea salt and black pepper

1 small bunch edible nasturtiums — stems removed

1　Pour a little olive oil into a large skillet placed over medium heat. Place the beet slices in the pan so that they barely overlap. (You will probably have to do this in 2 or 3 batches.) Drizzle a little of the white wine vinegar over the top and cook for 3–4 minutes, turning the beets once or twice. The beets should be just cooked through. Remove the pan from the heat, leaving the beets in the pan, covered for 3–4 minutes.

2　Pour a little olive oil into a large pan placed over medium-high heat. Add the sliced onions and cook for 5–6 minutes so that they are soft but not browned. Scatter the snap peas over the onions, stir and cook for 2 minutes. Toss in the pea tendrils and fava beans and cook, stirring frequently, for another minute or so. The tendrils will just start to wilt. As soon as they do, spoon all of this mixture into a salad bowl.

3　Combine the orange juice, fig balsamic vinegar and olive oil in a small bowl and whisk together well. Sprinkle in a good pinch of salt and some pepper and whisk once more to form a smooth emulsion.

4　Add the cooked beets to the salad bowl and drizzle with the vinaigrette. Toss to combine. Divide the salad between the salad plates and place the nasturtium flowers on top of each salad.

Fava Bean, Spring Pea and Almond Salad

I ate fava beans long before I ever prepared them. I think I would have appreciated them all the more. Yes, they are a bit of a chore to prepare, but I promise it's worth the effort. They are delicious. If you gather around a kitchen table with a few friends and good conversation, they'll be ready to cook in no time at all. If you have kids around, ask them to help, too. This is a springtime treat, filled with bright-green greens. You can add feta or goat cheese to this salad for a lovely variation.

Serves 8 people

Olive oil

4 shallots — peeled and thinly sliced

1 lb fava beans — shelled (you will need to remove the bean from the pod and then the outer shell of the fava bean — it's easier if you blanch them first for 2 minutes)

1 lb assorted spring peas — if using English peas, they will need to be shelled

Sea salt and black pepper

1 tablespoon Dijon mustard

3 tablespoons lemon olive oil

1 tablespoon Champagne vinegar or white wine vinegar

1/2 bunch chives — finely chopped

1/2 bunch mint leaves — try to use small leaves

8 oz assorted salad greens, including watercress if available

1/3 cup almonds

4 oz feta or goat cheese (optional)

1 Pour a little olive oil into a medium-sized skillet, placed over medium-high heat. Add the shallots and cook until soft and lightly golden (4–5 minutes).

2 Add the shelled fava beans and peas and cook for 2–3 minutes, so that they are warmed through. Season with salt and pepper and set aside.

3 Combine the mustard, olive oil and vinegar in a salad bowl, whisking together to form an emulsion. Place serving utensils over the vinaigrette. Place the assorted greens, herbs, almonds and pea-fava bean mixture in the salad bowl. When you are ready to serve, toss the salad so that all the ingredients are well combined.

Watercress and Spring Pea Salad

One of my cousins in France told me she thought it was odd that I put fruit in my salads. I asked her to taste the peach and tomato salad I made for her, and she has been a convert ever since. This salad has blueberries and mint, and a little zing in it. It's very refreshing!

Serves 8 people

Zest and juice of 1 lemon

3 tablespoons olive oil

Sea salt and black pepper

1 lb fava beans — shelled (you will need to remove the beans from the pods, and then the outer shell of the fava bean — it's easier if you blanch them first for 2 minutes)

1 lb English peas — shelled

2 bunches watercress leaves

2 good handfuls mint leaves — try to use just small leaves

1/2 bunch cilantro leaves

2 baskets blueberries

4 oz feta cheese — crumbled

1 Combine the olive oil with the lemon zest and juice, a pinch of salt and 4–5 grinds of black pepper in the bottom of a salad bowl. Whisk together briskly. Place salad utensils over the vinaigrette.

2 Pour a little olive oil (really just a touch) into a medium-sized skillet placed over medium heat. Add the peas and fava beans to the skillet and cook for no more than 2–3 minutes. Do not overcook them. Spoon the cooked peas and beans into the salad bowl, on top of the utensils. Place all the remaining ingredients in the bowl on top of the peas and fava beans.

3 When you are ready to serve the salad, toss gently so that everything is well combined.

Cherry, Pea and Fava Bean Salad

The fava bean and cherry seasons overlap for about four weeks, which doesn't give you much time to make this salad. You see the cherries but not the fava beans, then the beans but not the cherries. However, when you do get both of them together, they are magical. This salad is the essence of spring.

Serves 8 people

Olive oil

4 shallots — peeled
and sliced

1/2 lb English peas — shelled

1/2 lb snap peas — sliced
on a bias

1 lb fava beans — shelled
(you will need to remove
the beans from the pods,
and then the outer shell
of the fava bean — it's
easier if you blanch them
first for 2 minutes)

Sea salt and black pepper

1 lb cherries — pitted
and halved

Zest and juice of 1 lemon

1/2 cup basil leaves

1/2 cup mint leaves

1 Pour a little olive oil into a skillet placed over medium heat. Add the shallots and cook for 5 minutes. Add the peas, snap peas and fava beans, a pinch of salt and some pepper and cook for 3 minutes. Remove from the heat and set aside.

2 Pour 3 tablespoons olive oil into the bottom of a salad bowl and then whisk in the lemon zest and juice, a pinch of salt and some black pepper. Place salad utensils over the vinaigrette and then add the cherries to the bowl. Place the mint and basil leaves on top of the cherries and add the cooked peas and fava beans mixture to the bowl.

3 When you are ready to serve the salad, toss the ingredients well. You can make a different version using chives and cilantro leaves instead of the basil leaves.

LENTILS, POTATOES & ROASTED VEGETABLES

Lentils du Puy Salad with Spiced Greek Yogurt

—

Black Lentils with Roasted Tomatoes

—

Fingerling Potato and Bacon Salad

—

Smoked Salmon Salad

—

Grilled Zucchini and Tarragon Roasted Chicken Salad

Lentils du Puy Salad with Spiced Greek Yogurt

The French make a great deal of fuss about these lentils and just how good they are. I am a complete fan to the point where I don't really want to make any lentil dish without them. You may think that a lentil is a lentil is a lentil, but when it comes to these little slate green gems, that is not true. These are the *nec plus ultra* of lentils. That said, there's a recipe for black lentils on the next page, and actually they're pretty good, too — but I have to give the edge to these.

One of the best lentil salads I have ever had was in a little café in St. Tropez, which, unfortunately, no longer exists in its original incarnation. The lady who ran the restaurant knew her lentils. The salad was simple, served with a vinaigrette and some herbs. The lentils weren't goopy or mushy. You tasted each one. Perfect. My lentil salads aspire to that one.

Serves 8 people

2 cups Lentils du Puy
(French lentils — they are
small and dark green)

4 cups boiling water

3 bay leaves

Olive oil

2 medium red onions —
peeled and finely diced

2 cloves garlic — peeled and
minced

2 teaspoons Ras al Hanout

1 teaspoon curry powder

1 lb baby kale —
finely chopped

2 cups Greek yogurt

1/2 bunch Italian parsley
leaves

1/2 bunch chives —
finely chopped

Juice and zest of 1 lemon

Sea salt and black pepper

1 Place the lentils and bay leaves in a large saucepan filled with boiling water and cook for 20–30 minutes. They should be al dente. Drain and set aside.

2 Pour a little olive oil into a medium-sized skillet placed over medium-low heat. Add the onions, garlic, the Ras al Hanout and curry powder. Cook for 8–10 minutes until the onions are very soft and translucent. Add the chopped kale and cook until the kale has wilted, about 4-5 minutes. Set aside to cool.

3 Place the yogurt in a large salad bowl. Add the cooked onion-kale mixture and the herbs. Toss to coat well. Add the lentils, lemon juice, lemon zest, a good pinch of salt and some black pepper and toss again to combine.

Black Lentils with Roasted Tomatoes

Given how I feel about Lentils du Puy (see the previous recipe), I was a little skeptical the first time I tried black lentils. I am always happy to be proved wrong when it comes to culinary things. These were delicious. When you combine them with the roasted tomatoes, all the juice from the tomatoes mixes in with the lentils and creates a juicy sauce-cum-vinaigrette. All the fresh herbs add a nice balance to the earthy lentils. This is great dish to serve as part of a vegetarian meal or alongside some grilled fish or roast chicken.

Serves 8 people

1 ⅓ cups black lentils —
    rinsed well

5 cups hot water

1 lb small yellow tomatoes

Olive oil

Sea salt and black pepper

Juice and zest of 2 lemons

3 tablespoons olive oil

2 tablespoons chives —
    finely chopped

1 bunch green onions —
    ends trimmed and stalks
    cut into thin slices

1 tablespoon parsley — finely
    chopped

1   Preheat the oven to 350 degrees.

2   Pour the lentils and hot water into a large saucepan. Cover and simmer gently until the lentils are cooked, approximately 20 minutes. Taste them. They should be tender but not overly so. Drain the lentils.

3   Place the tomatoes in an ovenproof dish that is just large enough to hold them. Drizzle with some olive oil, and add a pinch of salt and some black pepper. Roast the tomatoes for 20–25 minutes. They will start to render juice and should get a little wrinkled.

4   Whisk the lemon juice, zest and olive oil together in a salad bowl. Add the cooked tomatoes (and all the juice they have rendered) and toss them gently in the vinaigrette. Stir in the cooked lentils. Sprinkle the chives, green onions and parsley over the salad and mix again to combine all of the ingredients.

Fingerling Potato and Bacon Salad

I like good homemade mayonnaise. It bears no resemblance to store-bought varieties. I have spent many hours carefully whisking in one drop of oil at a time to try and create the perfect mayo. There were times when I thought I would just make a mustard vinaigrette instead because I did not want the hassle (there's no denying that it usually is) of making homemade mayonnaise. No more! I came across a great trick on the internet. All you need is an immersion blender (sometimes they're called stick blenders). It is absolutely worth buying one of these, if only to make mayonnaise, but really because it makes blending soups so simple too. I could not believe how easy it was to make mayo — 1 minute at the most — and it is really amazing.

Serves 8 people

2 1/2 lbs fingerling potatoes — try to use different varieties

8 slices bacon

For the mayonnaise:

1 teaspoon Dijon mustard

1 egg yolk

2/3 cup olive oil

Juice of 1 lemon

1 tablespoon lemon basil leaves — chopped

1 teaspoon lemon thyme leaves

1 teaspoon chives — chopped

1 tablespoon parsley — chopped

Pinch of sea salt

1 Place all the potatoes in a large saucepan of boiling water with a pinch of salt and cook until tender but not falling apart. Drain, let cool, cut into 1/2-inch thick slices (if some of the fingerlings are small, leave them whole) and place them in a salad bowl.

2 Cook the bacon in a large skillet or under a broiler until crispy. Drain on a paper towel until cool, and then chop into small pieces.

3 To make the mayonnaise, place the mustard and egg yolk into a tall plastic cylinder or beaker — it should not be too wide. Next, add the olive oil and lemon juice. Finally, add all of the remaining ingredients to the beaker. Place the immersion blender in the beaker so that it touches the bottom. Run the immersion blender until you have a thick mayonnaise. You will have to tilt the blender a little to incorporate all the oil. Taste the finished mayonnaise. If it's very thick, add some lemon juice or a tablespoon of water and blend again.

4 Spoon the herb mayonnaise over the potatoes, add the bacon and toss to combine. This is great for a picnic or a barbecue.

Smoked Salmon Salad

This is another one of those salads that came about when I had bits and pieces left in the fridge — a couple of slices of smoked salmon, some salmon filet left over from dinner the night before and some little potatoes. I decide to chop up everything and mix it together, and this was the result — a spin on a Salade Niçoise.

Serves 8 people

½ lb fingerling potatoes

1 tablespoon Dijon mustard

¼ cup olive oil

1 tablespoon white wine vinegar or Champagne vinegar

Sea salt and black pepper

¾ lb smoked salmon filet or trout

¼ lb smoked salmon — sliced into small pieces.

2 bunches watercress — stems removed

¼ cup fresh dill — finely chopped

1 bunch chives — finely chopped

2 tablespoons fresh fennel bulb — finely diced

Zest and juice of 1 lemon

1. Place the fingerling potatoes in a saucepan filled with boiling water and cook until just tender. Drain and set aside. Slice them when they have cooled a little.

2. Whisk together the mustard, olive oil and vinegar in a large salad bowl. Add a pinch of salt and some pepper. Place salad utensils over the vinaigrette. Break the salmon filet into pieces and place them on top of the utensils. Add the smoked salmon, watercress, herbs, fennel, lemon zest and juice on top of the salmon filet pieces, and then add the warm fingerling potatoes to the salad bowl.

3. When you are ready to serve the salad, toss to combine the ingredients.

Grilled Zucchini and Tarragon Roasted Chicken Salad

Poulet a l'estragon (tarragon chicken) was — actually still is — one of the dishes that I always looked forward to when visiting France. It's classic bistro fare, or *cuisine bourgeoise*. In other words, good home cooking.

Deft use of tarragon is key, as the slightly anise-flavored herb can be overpowering if used in large quantities. I always think of it as the quintessential French herb. It's used in a number of classic sauces, Béarnaise being the most well known.

This salad pairs moist tarragon roasted chicken with grilled zucchini and a mustardy vinaigrette.

Serves 8 people

3 ½ lbs whole chicken

2 yellow onions — peeled and thinly sliced

Olive oil

4 sprigs tarragon to roast with the chicken, plus the leaves from 1-2 more sprigs for the finished salad

Sea salt and black pepper

1 tablespoon Dijon mustard

4 tablespoons olive oil

1 tablespoon tarragon vinegar or white wine vinegar

5 zucchini — ends trimmed away and then sliced on a bias

1 Preheat the oven to 400 degrees.

2 Cover the bottom of a roasting pan with the sliced onions. Place the chicken on top and drizzle with a little olive oil. Tuck the tarragon sprigs around the chicken. Sprinkle a little salt and then grind some black pepper over the chicken. Roast for 90 minutes.

3 Spoon the mustard into the bottom of a large salad bowl. Pour in the olive oil and vinegar and whisk together well. It will look like mayonnaise. Place the serving utensils on top of the vinaigrette.

4 Pour a little olive oil into a large mixing bowl and add all the zucchini slices, a pinch of salt and some pepper. Toss to coat.

5 Place a grill pan on top of a stove and heat until it gets nice and hot. Grill the zucchini slices so that they are just cooked. Turn them after 2 minutes. You may have to do this in batches as all the slices may not fit on the grill in one layer. Add the grilled zucchini to the salad bowl.

6 Place the cooked chicken on a cutting board and let rest for 10 minutes before carving. Carve the chicken, removing all the meat and chopping it up into bite-sized pieces. Add the chicken pieces, the sliced roasted onions from the roasting pan, and the fresh tarragon leaves to the bowl.

7 When you are ready to serve, toss the ingredients well so that everything gets nicely coated with the vinaigrette.

MUSHROOMS

Warm Mushroom
and White
Asparagus Salad

~

Wild Mushroom
and Pea Salad

~

Wild Mushroom
Crostini with an
Arugula Salad

~

Salade des
Cousinades

Warm Mushroom and White Asparagus Salad

This salad contains two of my favorite ingredients — white asparagus and wild mushrooms. If the wild mushrooms happen to be chanterelles, even better. Honestly, there are few things that are more mouth watering than the aroma of sizzling butter in a pan with sliced mushrooms cooking in it. Sometimes I'll cook a few mushrooms to add to a green salad or put on some toast with a piece of goat cheese. I love their earthy flavors. White asparagus have a herbaceous quality to them. They balance the rustic qualities of the mushrooms in this salad. It's a dish I look forward to every spring as we emerge from winter.

Serves 8 people

2 lbs white asparagus —
  carefully peeled, tips cut
  off, and stems cut on a
  bias in 1-inch pieces

Olive oil

2 shallots — peeled and
  finely sliced

1 tablespoon butter

1 1/2 lbs assorted wild
  mushrooms — cleaned
  and sliced

1 bunch chives —
  finely chopped

For the vinaigrette:

1 teaspoon Dijon mustard

3 tablespoons olive oil

1 tablespoon vinegar

Sea salt and black pepper

1 Place the asparagus in a steamer or in a large pan of lightly salted boiling water and cook for 6–7 minutes until just al dente. Remove, drain and set aside.

2 While the asparagus are cooking, pour a little olive oil into a large skillet placed over medium-high heat. Add the shallots and cook until just golden, about 3 minutes. Add a tablespoon of butter and then the sliced mushrooms. Cook until golden brown. Sprinkle in the chives. Cook for 1 minute more and then set aside.

3 For the vinaigrette, combine the mustard, olive oil and vinegar in a large salad bowl and whisk until you have an emulsion. Add in a pinch of salt and some black pepper. Place serving utensils over the vinaigrette and then add the asparagus and mushrooms to the bowl, on top of the utensils. When you are ready to serve, toss the salad carefully and divide between eight plates.

Wild Mushroom and Pea Salad

This is a fresh, crunchy salad with lots of tasty, golden mushrooms in it. You can use any blue cheese — I like to use a creamy Stilton — and any combination of mushrooms. If you don't like blue cheese, use feta. Try to serve this whilst the ingredients are still warm as the cheese melts slightly and makes it even more delectable.

Serves 8 people

1 tablespoon butter

1 lb assorted wild mushrooms
    — cleaned and sliced

Olive oil

1 lb English peas, snap peas
    (cut on a bias), green
    peas

For the vinaigrette:

¼ cup olive oil

1 tablespoon pear
    Champagne vinegar

Sea salt and black pepper

2 tablespoons chives —
    finely chopped

1 tablespoon blue cheese

1 Place the butter in a large pan over medium-high heat and add the sliced mushrooms. Cook until just browned. Remove the mushrooms from the pan before they start to render any water. Set aside on a plate.

2 Return the pan to the heat and add a little olive oil. Add all the peas and cook for 3–4 minutes so that they are cooked through but still somewhat firm.

3 In a large salad bowl, whisk together the olive oil and vinegar. Stir in some salt and pepper and all the chives. Place serving utensils over the vinaigrette and add the blue cheese, wild mushrooms and peas on top. When you are ready to serve the salad, toss to combine the ingredients well.

Wild Mushroom Crostini with an Arugula Salad

I once was caught in an early evening downpour in Venice. To avoid getting completely soaked, I ducked into a minuscule *bacaro*, one of their local wine bars. Everyone else had the same idea, and the place was packed. We were all crammed in along the small zinc bar on which were displayed a dazzling array of *cicheti* — Venetian tapas. Small glasses of wine were soon being handed across the bar along with the assorted nibbles. One in particular stands out — small toasts with sautéed porcini. Maybe it was the atmosphere, the flirtatious barman or the fading light across the canal, but that little toast was truly marvelous.

This salad is a nod to that day — an arugula salad — also something I ate everywhere in Italy, and those scrumptious toasts.

Serves 8 people

3 shallots — finely diced

2 tablespoons butter

1 lb assorted wild
  mushrooms — sliced

1 teaspoon mushroom truffle
  tapenade (available at
  gourmet grocery markets)

1/2 cup black olives — pitted
  and coarsely chopped

Baguette or whole wheat
  bread — sliced and
  toasted (you will need
  three small slices per
  person)

Butter

For the arugula salad:

1/4 cup olive oil

1 tablespoon red wine
  vinegar

Sea salt and black pepper

1/2 bunch chives — finely
  chopped

6 oz arugula — washed and
  any large stems removed

1 Sauté the shallots in a little butter in a medium-sized skillet until they are soft and golden. Add the mushrooms and cook until soft and lightly browned, about 3–4 minutes. Add the mushroom truffle tapenade and black olives. Stir to combine and remove from the heat.

2 Butter the toasts and then spoon a little of the mushroom mixture on top. Serve hot!

3 To make the arugula salad, whisk together the olive oil, vinegar, a large pinch of salt and some fresh black pepper in a medium-sized salad bowl. Place serving utensils over the vinaigrette. Place the arugula and chives on top of the utensils.

4 When you are ready to serve, use the utensils to toss the salad. Divide the salad equally between eight salad plates and serve the mushroom crostini with it.

Salade des Cousinades

Every few years, my family in France gets together for an event we call *Les Cousinades*, literally "the cousins' get-together." Each event is organized by one cousin, usually in an area known for very good food. We are a family that is, for the most part, somewhat obsessed with anything culinary. On one of these family pilgrimages, 55 of us (yes, all related to each other) took over a restaurant in Sarlat in the Périgord-Dordogne region, a town known for its golden-colored architecture and all things related to duck and cèpes (porcini). Lunch began with a *Salade aux Cèpes.* The mushrooms and accompanying potatoes had been sautéed in duck fat. It was very good. This is my version of that salad, a tribute to my cousins.

Serves 8 people

For the vinaigrette:

2 tablespoons olive oil

1 tablespoon truffle oil

1 tablespoon red wine vinegar or Jerez vinegar

Large pinch of sea salt

Freshly ground black pepper

For the salad:

1/2 lb fresh or 4 oz dried porcini mushrooms

1 1/2 lbs wild mushrooms — finely sliced

8 oz small new potatoes or fingerling potatoes

2 tablespoons duck fat

2 tablespoons butter

4 oz mache salad greens

1 bunch chives — finely chopped

Sea salt and black pepper

1 Combine all of the vinaigrette ingredients in the bottom of a large salad bowl and whisk together until you have a smooth vinaigrette. If you like the vinaigrette to be a little sweeter, add a little more of the vinegar. Place the serving utensils over the vinaigrette.

2 Soak the dried porcini mushrooms in a small bowl of boiling hot water, or vegetable stock, for 20 minutes. (Omit this step if using fresh mushrooms.) Drain the mushrooms.

3 While the mushrooms are soaking, cook the potatoes in a large saucepan of boiling salted water for about 10–15 minutes. Drain, then slice thinly.

4 Pour a little duck fat into a large sauté pan and sauté the sliced potatoes until golden brown on both sides. Spoon the cooked potatoes into the salad bowl.

5 Add the butter to the same sauté pan, and cook the mushrooms (each variety separately). They will only need a few minutes each. Add them to the salad bowl.

6 Place the mache and chives on top of the potatoes and mushrooms. Toss the salad when you are ready to serve.

NECTARINES, PEACHES & PLUMS

Nectarine, Buffalo
Mozzarella and
Fennel Salad

—

Plum and
Watercress Salad

—

Herb Salad with
Late Summer Peaches,
Goat Cheese and
Blistered Almonds

—

Mache, Mint and
Pluot Salad

—

White Nectarine
Carpaccio with a
Microgreen Salad

—

Peach, Melon and
Prosciutto Salad

—

Grilled Peach,
Heirloom Tomato and
Arugula Salad

Nectarine, Buffalo Mozzarella and Fennel Salad

Many years ago on a trip to Italy, I had the ubiquitous tomato and mozzarella salad. I was going to order something else, but the waiter insisted that I have the salad as the mozzarella had just arrived and was fresh. I realized, in hindsight, that I had no clue what he meant by "fresh." He meant made-in-the-last-12-hours fresh. The plate arrived with some sliced tomatoes and a whole mozzarella in the middle. A bottle of olive oil was placed on the table. There was also some salt and pepper — nothing else. This did not look promising. Then I took a bite. The waiter had been watching me. I looked at him in amazement. He just nodded and smiled. I have never — to this day — tasted mozzarella like that. It was rich, creamy and soft, yet just firm enough to hold together. This was mozzarella perfection.

Don't get me wrong, I have found good mozzarella since then, and when I do, I like to tear it into small pieces and add it to all sorts of salads. This is one of them.

Serves 8 people

3 tablespoons olive oil

1 tablespoon Champagne
    vinegar

Pinch of sea salt

Black pepper

4–6 medium-sized ripe
    nectarines — pitted
    and sliced

1 lb fresh buffalo mozzarella
    — gently torn into bite-
    sized pieces

1 fennel bulb — cut in half
    and then thinly sliced

2 white endives — root
    end trimmed and leaves
    separated

1/2 bunch chives —
    finely chopped

1/2 bunch dill —
    finely chopped

1 In a medium-sized, shallow salad bowl, whisk together the olive oil, vinegar, salt and pepper. Place salad utensils over the vinaigrette.

2 Place all the remaining ingredients on top of the salad utensils. When you are ready to serve the salad, remove the utensils and toss all the ingredients together gently.

Plum and Watercress Salad

I have a prolific plum tree in my garden. This year we had another bumper crop, and after two huge batches of jam, I still had plums all over the kitchen. We used them in everything — with roasted chicken, clafoutis, plum cake and salads. This was one of the favorites from the summer.

Serves 8 people

¼ cup olive oil

½ bunch cilantro — chopped

½ bunch basil — chopped

Juice and zest of 1 lemon

Juice and zest of 1 lime

Sea salt

Black pepper

16 plums — pitted and thinly sliced

8 oz watercress

2 oz mixed nuts (pistachios, macadamias, walnuts, almonds) — chopped and then dry roasted in a pan for 2 minutes

2 oz feta cheese — crumbled

1 Place the olive oil, cilantro, basil, lemon zest and juice, lime zest and juice, a pinch of salt and 3–4 twists of pepper in a blender. Puree until smooth.

2 Pour the herb vinaigrette into the bottom of a large salad bowl and then place serving utensils on top of the vinaigrette.

3 Place the watercress and plum slices on top of the serving utensils.

4 When you are ready to serve the salad, toss to combine well. Divide the salad equally between the plates and then sprinkle the chopped nuts and the feta over the top of each salad.

Herb Salad with Late Summer Peaches, Goat Cheese and Blistered Almonds

Every autumn, the city of Santa Barbara, California, is home to the SOL (sustainable, organic, local) Food Festival. Imagine a park filled with thousands of SOL food enthusiasts, meandering past turkeys, chickens in very stylish coops, displays of everything from organic gardening to organic wines, participating in workshops or watching demonstrations. It's the brainchild of four dedicated people who passionately believe that food should be grown naturally. I've been thrilled to participate in this event since it first began, usually doing demonstrations and being a judge for their "Iron Chef" inspired competition. Last year, I taught a hands-on class showcasing produce from local farms. This is the salad I created for the event.

Serves 8 people

For the vinaigrette:

4 tablespoons olive oil

Juice of 2 lemons

10 cherry tomatoes

Pinch of sea salt

Freshly ground black pepper

For the salad:

6 oz mixed salad greens with lots of herbs — try to include some purple basil and dill if possible

1 tablespoon finely chopped chives

6–8 peaches — cut into thin slices (if they are large, 4 will suffice)

8 oz goat cheese — cut into thin slices

4 oz salted almonds

1 Whisk together the olive oil and lemon juice in a salad bowl. Using a fork, crush the tomatoes in a small bowl. Add them to the vinaigrette. Add the salt and pepper and stir to combine. Place salad utensils on top of the vinaigrette.

2 Place all of the remaining ingredients in the salad bowl, on top of the salad utensils. When ready to serve, gently toss the salad so that the peach slices and goat cheese slices stay intact.

Mache, Mint and Pluot Salad

I am a fairly recent convert to pluots. I used to regard them as some sort of weird hybrid thing. I preferred plums to be plums and apricots, well, apricots. It was only when a local farmer urged me to overcome my reticence and actually try one that I realized the error of my ways. The fruit was delicious — a true reflection of its parental roots. When cut open, pluots reveal an array of jewel-toned colors and have marvelous names such as *Dapple Dandy, Flavor Grenade* and *Raspberry Jewel*. They make incredible jams. They also add sweet floral notes to salads.

Serves 8 people

For the vinaigrette:

Juice of 2 large lemons
(or 3 small ones)

Coarse sea salt

1/2 tablespoon honey

1/3 cup olive oil

Freshly ground pepper

For the salad:

2 oz pine nuts

1/2 teaspoon fennel seeds

1/2 teaspoon mustard seeds

1/2 teaspoon coriander seeds

8 oz mache (lamb's lettuce)

8–10 pluots (use different
varieties) — sliced

2 handfuls golden raisins

1 small bunch mint leaves

1 bunch chives —
finely chopped

1 Combine all the vinaigrette ingredients in the bottom of a large salad bowl and whisk together vigorously.

2 Put the pine nuts, fennel, mustard and coriander seeds in a small skillet placed over medium heat. Toast them until the nuts turn a pale golden color and the spices release their fragrance. Add the mixture to the vinaigrette and combine, and then place salad servers over the vinaigrette.

3 Place the remaining salad ingredients on top of the servers, ensuring that the greens stay out of the vinaigrette (otherwise the mache will get soggy).

4 Toss the salad well just before serving. Distribute evenly between eight salad plates.

White Nectarine Carpaccio with a Microgreen Salad

Microgreens are tiny versions of various lettuces, herbs and greens that are harvested when they are very small — usually no more than an inch or so in height. They are packed with nutrients and have the distinct flavor of the more mature plant. First used in high-end restaurants, they are now more widely available for commercial use. They are also apparently easy to grow. This is going to be my next garden project.

I like using a mix of slightly spicy microgreens containing baby arugula. They complement the sweet nectarines. You can also use white peaches in this salad.

Serves 8 people

8 white nectarines

6 oz microgreens

3–4 sprigs lemon thyme leaves — finely chopped

½ bunch chives — finely chopped

1 large handful basil leaves (different varieties if possible)

⅓ cup extra virgin olive oil

1 ½ tablespoons pear Champagne vinegar or other white wine vinegar

Zest of 1 lemon

Sea salt and black pepper

1   Thinly slice the nectarines into disks — when you get to the pit, cut carefully around it so that you can take it out without splitting the nectarine in two.

2   Place the slices onto salad plates so that they overlap slightly and cover the entire surface of each plate. Work from the outside of the plate toward the center. It should look like one or two concentric circles.

3   Combine the microgreens with the thyme and chives in a medium-sized bowl. Mound the microgreens in the middle of each plate on top of the nectarines. Insert the basil leaves between the nectarine slices.

4   Combine the olive oil, vinegar and lemon zest in a small bowl and whisk together to form an emulsion. Add a pinch of salt and some pepper. Drizzle a little of the vinaigrette over the nectarines and the microgreens on each plate. Serve immediately.

Peach, Melon and Prosciutto Salad

As a small child in Provence, I ate melons that were sweet, juicy, intensely floral and tasted of honey. We would pick them surreptitiously from the field neighboring our farmhouse. They would be served with prosciutto on rustic wooden plates. It was one of the hallmarks of summer. Whenever I come across one of these melons, I am transported back to that field and to the markets of Provence. Evidently, that sensation is hereditary. On one of the photo shoot days for *Salade*, whilst I was preparing this salad, my daughter came into the kitchen and tasted a piece of the melon. She took one bite and exclaimed, "This makes me feel like I'm in France!"

Serves 8 people

1 Tuscan melon (sometimes called Tuscan cantaloupe) — halved, seeded, peeled and cut into thin slices

4 yellow freestone peaches — halved, pitted and cut into thin slices

4 white freestone peaches — halved, pitted and cut into thin slices

16–20 slices prosciutto

1 large handful arugula

1 bunch chives — finely chopped

4 tablespoons olive oil — use a good, fruity oil

Sea salt and freshly ground black pepper

4 oz mozzarella, goat cheese or feta cheese (optional)

1 Arrange all the melon and peach slices on a large platter or on individual plates, alternating the fruit. Dot the surface with the prosciutto. Sprinkle the chives and arugula leaves over the top and drizzle with olive oil. Add a pinch of salt and some black pepper.

You can also serve this with fresh mozzarella, goat cheese or feta.

Grilled Peach, Heirloom Tomato and Arugula Salad

This is a variation of the salad that is on the cover of my *Summer* cookbook. I love the combination of tomatoes and peaches and have made many versions of that salad. I particularly like this one. Grilling the peaches intensifies the sugars in the fruit and gives them a slightly charred-caramel taste. The sweetness of the fruit is delicious against the peppery arugula.

Serves 8 people

For the pesto vinaigrette:

4 tablespoons olive oil

Juice and zest of 2 lemons

1 large handful arugula —
   roughly chopped

1 cup basil leaves —
   roughly chopped

Pinch of coarse sea salt

For the salad:

2 lbs large heirloom
   tomatoes —
   approximately the same
   size as the peaches,
   halved and cut into
   wedges

4–6 large peaches —
   halved, pitted and
   cut into wedges

2 tablespoons olive oil

Sea salt and black pepper

1 Place all of the ingredients for the pesto in a blender and blend until you have a thick vinaigrette.

2 Place the tomatoes into a large salad bowl.

3 Place a grill pan over medium-high heat.

4 Place the peaches into a separate bowl and add the olive oil. Toss so that the peaches are coated. Sprinkle a little salt and pepper over the peaches. Toss again. Place the peaches on the grill and cook for 90 seconds. Carefully turn the peaches onto the other side and cook for 1 minute more.

5 Carefully remove the peaches from the grill and add them to the tomatoes.

6 Drizzle the pesto vinaigrette over the salad, toss carefully, so as not to break the fruit. Serve immediately.

TOMATOES

Heirloom Tomato
Salad

~

Pampelone Salad

~

Yellow Tomato and
Purple Basil Salad

~

Roasted Tomato and
Olive Salad

~

Field Greens with
Savory Tomatoes
and Warm Buffalo
Mozzarella

~

Kale and Chard
Salad with Sautéed
Cherry Tomatoes

~

Green Tomato and
Grilled Zucchini
Salad

Heirloom Tomato Salad

One of the great pleasures of summer is the plethora of tomatoes that flood the farmers' markets. This salad is a celebration of those tomatoes.

Serves 8 to 10 people

8 large heirloom tomatoes (different varieties) — thinly sliced horizontally

8–10 small heirloom tomatoes or cherry tomatoes — thinly sliced horizontally

3 tablespoons olive oil

1 tablespoon white wine vinegar

Large pinch of coarse sea salt or flake salt such as Maldon or Murray River

Black pepper

2 tablespoons chives — finely chopped

1 Lay all the tomato slices, slightly overlapping one another, on a large platter. Place the small slices on top of the larger ones and alternate the colors.

2 Combine the olive oil, vinegar, salt and pepper in a small bowl and whisk together. Drizzle the vinaigrette all over the tomatoes. Sprinkle the salad with the chives and serve.

Pampelone Salad

There is a restaurant on the beach near my father's house in France. It opened in 1955 and has been run by the same family ever since. The blue Provençal tablecloth-covered tables are set outside under large white awnings. We always go there for lunch on the first day we arrive in Provence. They have been making a tomato and goat cheese salad served with a thick mayonnaise and fresh mint for as long as I can remember; and it's the first dish I eat whenever I return to this charming restaurant. This is my version of that salad.

Serves 8 people

16 medium-sized firm ripe tomatoes (Romas or heirlooms of your choice) — thinly sliced

9 oz goat cheese log (it should be quite firm) — sliced into thin rounds

1 tablespoon Dijon mustard

3 tablespoons olive oil

1 tablespoon vinegar

Sea salt and black pepper to taste

20 mint leaves

20 basil leaves

1 Arrange the sliced tomatoes and sliced goat cheese alternating between the two in overlapping rows.

2 Place the mustard into a small bowl. Pour the olive oil and vinegar into the bowl, and whisk until the vinaigrette is homogeneous. Add salt and pepper to taste.

3 Pour the vinaigrette over the middle of the tomatoes to form a thick ribbon.

4 Insert the mint and basil leaves between the tomatoes and basil.

Yellow Tomato and Purple Basil Salad

This salad came about because of the colorful sunflower yellow tomatoes, and the purple basil that was in a basket alongside, that I saw at a local farm stand. The colors were brilliant together, so I had to try mixing the two and, honestly, how can you go wrong with tomatoes and basil? This salad is easy to make, gorgeous to look at, fresh and bursting with flavor.

Serves 8 people

3 tablespoons olive oil

1 tablespoon white wine vinegar

Zest and juice of 1 lemon

1 1/2 lbs small and large yellow tomatoes — halved and the larger ones cut into wedges

1 small bunch purple basil leaves

Sea salt and freshly ground black pepper

1 Combine the olive oil, vinegar, lemon zest and juice in a large salad bowl. Whisk together to form a smooth emulsion. Place salad utensils over the vinaigrette.

2 Add all the tomatoes and basil on top of the utensils. When you are ready to serve the salad, toss it gently so that everything is well combined. Sprinkle some coarse sea salt or flake salt and some freshly ground pepper over the salad.

Roasted Tomato and Olive Salad

I love slowly roasted cherry tomatoes. I use them in lots of dishes from pasta to crostini. Their flavor is intensified and they become rich and juicy. Add them to any salad, and it transforms the vinaigrette as the juices from the tomatoes melt in with the salad. The olives are a tasty, salty counterpoint.

Serves 8 people

1 lb small tomatoes

Olive oil

1 teaspoon Herbes de Provence

8 oz baby arugula

6 oz black olives — pitted

1 bunch chives — finely chopped

For the vinaigrette:

¼ cup olive oil

1 tablespoon red wine vinegar

½ bunch basil — roughly chopped

Zest of 1 lemon

1 tablespoon chives — roughly chopped

1 Preheat the oven to 275 degrees.

2 Place the tomatoes in a small baking dish. Pour a little olive oil over the tomatoes and then sprinkle the Herbes de Provence over the top. Shake the pan to coat well. Roast the tomatoes for 2 hours.

3 For the vinaigrette, place the olive oil, vinegar, basil, lemon zest and chopped chives in a blender or food processor. Blend until you have a thick vinaigrette. It should have consistency that is lighter than a pesto. Pour the vinaigrette into a salad bowl. Place utensils over the vinaigrette. Add the arugula on top of the utensils.

4 Add the cooked tomatoes and olives to the salad bowl. When you are ready to serve the salad, toss the ingredients so that everything is well combined. Divide equally between the salad plates and sprinkle the chives over the top.

Green Tomato and Grilled Zucchini Salad

This salad is in honor of the first green zebra tomatoes I managed to grow. I was so excited by my little crop! I ate one straight off the vine, still warm from the sun. With the rest, I made this salad. Unfortunately, it may have been the only one of the summer, as I think my poor tomato plant exhausted itself in that first bloom. I have all sorts of ideas for the next batch. They will have to go into the next book!

Serves 8 people

2 lbs zucchini — ends trimmed and thinly sliced on a bias

Olive oil

Sea salt and black pepper

Juice and zest of 2 lemons

Juice and zest of 1 lime

2 lbs green tomatoes — cut into wedges

1 bunch chives — finely chopped

1 Pour a little olive oil into a large bowl. Add the zucchini slices, a good pinch of salt and 4–5 grinds of pepper. Toss to coat well.

2 Combine 3 tablespoons olive oil, lemon juice and zest and lime juice and zest in a large salad bowl. Place serving utensils over the vinaigrette. Add the sliced tomatoes and chives to the bowl.

3 Place a cast-iron grill pan over high heat. Grill the zucchini in batches for 2–3 minutes on each side until they are just cooked through. As each batch of zucchini is cooked, add it to the salad bowl. Once all the zucchini are cooked, toss the salad gently so that everything is well combined.

Suppliers & Sources

I am often asked where I buy my produce, fish, meat, flowers and wine. These purveyors, shops and markets are the ones I use whilst in California. They have all proven to be reliable, and I heartily recommend them.

SANTA BARBARA

CHEESE

C'est Cheese
www.cestcheese.com
(805) 965-0318

The best local shop for exquisite cheeses and gourmet items run by a charming couple, Kathryn and Michael Graham.

HERBS AND SPICES

Pascale's Kitchen
www.pascaleskitchen.com
(805) 965-5112

A great resource for exotic salts, herbs, spice blends and olive oils and beautiful kitchen items.

MEAT

Aside from the farmers' market, where you can get great local organic meat, there are a number of local stores, including Whole Foods Market, which carry locally raised meat products.

PATISSERIE

Renaud's Patisserie and Bistro
www.renaudsbakery.com
(805) 569-2400

There are croissants, and then there are Renaud's croissants — truly some of the best-tasting confections and macarons. This charming patisserie, owned by Renaud and Nicole Gonthier, is located in Loreto Plaza.

PRODUCE

Santa Barbara's Farmers Market
www.sbfarmersmarket.org
(805) 962-5354

At the market, I would highly recommend the following farms:

BD's Earthtrine Farms
(805) 640-1423

Fragrant herbs and wonderful vegetables.

Fairview Gardens
www.fairviewgardens.org
Great local organic farm.

Fat Uncle Farms
www.fatunclefarms.com

They have THE most incredible blistered almonds. Worth driving a long way to find them.

Peacock Farms
www.peacockfamilyfarms.com

Superb eggs, persimmons, tomatoes and dried fruit.

Pudwill Farms
(805) 268-4536

Great berries and figs.

Roots Organic Farm
Spectacular vegetables abound at this stand.

The Garden of .....
For the most beautiful and flavorful lettuce, herbs, leeks and tomatoes.

Mesa Produce
(805) 962-1645

This store is an excellent source for locally-farmed organic produce.

SEAFOOD

Kanaloa Seafood
www.kanaloa.com
1-888-KANALOA

Located on Gutierrez Street, Kanaloa offers the best, most varied and freshest seafood available.

Santa Barbara Fish Market
www.sbfish.com
(805) 965 9564

Excellent local market at the harbor where you can buy fresh fish that have come right off the local boats.

WINERIES

Santa Barbara County is home to many wonderful wineries that produce world-class vintages. Here are some of my favorites:

Alma Rosa Winery
www.almarosawinery.com

Buttonwood Farm and Winery
www.buttonwoodwinery.com

Riverbench Winery
www.riverbench.com

Zaca Mesa Winery
www.zacamesa.com

LOS ANGELES

BREAD

La Brea Bakery
www.labreabakery.com
(323) 939-6813

Open since 1989, America's most widely recognized artisan bakery sells delicious loaves from its original location on South La Brea and also nationwide.

CHEESE

The Cheese Store
www.cheesestorebh.com
(310) 278-2855

The best cheese shop in Los Angeles, with more than 400 fabulous cheeses and other delicious culinary products.

PRODUCE & FLOWERS

Santa Monica's Wednesday Farmers Market
www.santa-monica.org/farmers_market

The now-famous market is one of the largest in California and supplies many of Los Angeles's great restaurants. Worth a trip just to discover all sorts of seasonal goodies.

One of my favorite vendors there is **Windrose Farms**

www.windrosefarm.org

Fragrant heirloom tomatoes, squash, heirloom spuds and wonderful apples.

SEAFOOD

Santa Monica Seafood
www.santamonicaseafood.com
(310) 393-5244

A wonderful seafood store that supplies many of the top restaurants in Southern California. Their retail outlet is spectacular.

Index

Acknowledgments

This beautiful, colorful book came about with the help of a team of very dedicated people, a team that has supported, encouraged and nurtured me. I am hugely indebted and enormously grateful for their help and all myriad creative talents.

My first thank you goes to Mike Verbois, who photographed every salad. We spent months working on this project with 100 full-page images to shoot. When I looked at the shot list on the first day, the reality of just how big this project was hit me like the proverbial ton of bricks. We soon settled into our usual easy working rhythm and you created beautiful shot after beautiful shot. I am hugely grateful, Mike, for your exacting eye, precise attention to detail and patience. The book is stunning, Mike. Merci!

Next I would like to thank Judi Muller. This is the sixth book we have worked on together, and I am profoundly grateful for your wonderful design talents. This book marks a departure from the "seasons" and I have watched with pleasure the unfolding design of this new project. Thank you for making this volume so appealing, beautiful and so appetizing. It is truly a delight to work with you.

To Ruth Verbois for — as always — handling all the details for the publication of my books with grace, efficiency and your lovely smile. I am truly grateful for all of your help with all of these projects.

To Susan Noble, a thousand thank you's for once again casting your fine eye over the text and for finding the impossible! I appreciate *all* of your many efforts on my behalf.

To Shukri Farhad, I say thank you once again for all you do on my behalf. You handle everything with such aplomb! This book will mark ten years since we began working together, and I deeply appreciate all that you and M27 have done for me. It has been an exciting, challenging at times, and hugely satisfying creative voyage. May our journey continue for many years and many books to come.

Joan Tapper, I always enjoy our grammatical bantering and thank you once again for your exacting eye and painstaking attention to detail throughout.

To everyone at M27 Editions it goes without saying that this book (indeed all the books) would not have come to fruition without you. I am so very thankful for your continued support, energy and enthusiasm.

Nancy Oster, thank you for casting your most excellent culinary and editorial eye over this text and for giving me your feedback. It is — as always — a pleasure to work with you!

Sherry Mannello, what can I say, Sherry? You are a marvel, indefatigable and were ever-present through every day of the shoot, all my events and classes. Merci, merci for all your help, once again, with this project and all the times we have worked together. I am so thankful for your friendship and grateful for your massive efforts on my behalf.

Harriet Eckstein, words fail me here. There are so many things I have to say a gargantuan thank you for, the very least of which is the copy of the *Chicago Manual of Style,* which I secretly know you gave to me to thwart my irritating British spelling and punctuation. I am of course eternally grateful for ALL you have done, your endless support, and for reading every single page of this book and correcting the aforementioned quirky text.

Nancy Whetter, you are truly an inspiration. In the midst of everything, you took time to read this book, to correct — in your most gentle way — the text, to lend your support and to help with so many aspects of the photo shoots. I am so touched by your encouragement and your steadfast belief in this project and in me and am humbled by your efforts on my behalf. Merci.

Creating this book — as with all such projects — takes time and energy. Needless to say that it impacts everyone around me. To my children, Olivia and Alexandre, I say *encore merci.* Once again you absorbed the daily shoot routine into your lives and were uncomplaining throughout the project. I hugely appreciate your patience and encouragement. You are both fabulous!

To my parents, you astound me. You are always there, always present with your support and help, giving moral boosts when needed, and cheering me on. I could not have done any of this without you. *Encore, encore, mille fois merci.*